Pure As He Is Pure

My Struggle With Homosexuality

By

Chancellor Carlyle Roberts, II

ISBN: 1-4033-1704-6

This book is printed on acid free paper.

1stBooks - rev. 04/05/02

All scripture references, unless otherwise stated, are from the King James Version.
All definitions of Hebrew and Greek words are from Strong's Exhaustive Concordance of the Bible.

TABLE OF CONTENTS

INTRODUCTION

"God hates fags. They deserve to die. Their perverted, wicked lifestyle is responsible for the destruction of entire civilizations. They prey on innocent children. Homosexuals have brought God's judgment on America and that's why terrorists crashed into the World Trade Center and the Pentagon on September 11, 2001." Does any of this sound familiar? How often have you heard such things? Considering that such pronouncements have come quite frequently from the mouths and pens of Christians, it's clear that homosexuality incites strong emotions within the body of Christ. Perhaps no other issue in the Church has been so controversial, so polarizing, as homosexuality. Is homosexuality a choice? Is it a sin? Is it caused? Is a person born homosexual? Did God create some people to be homosexual? What does the Bible really say about homosexuality, if anything at all? Can a homosexual change? If so, must a homosexual change? If he can and must change, into what must he change? The debate rages on. This issue has torn apart families and divided congregations. The words of James 3:10 are hauntingly applicable to many believers when it comes to the subject of homosexuality: "Out of the same mouth proceedeth blessing and cursing." This issue, perhaps more than any other, has resulted in Christians behaving in an unchristian manner. To echo the words of James 3:10, "My brethren, these things ought not so to be."

There are many books in print about homosexuality. They range the entire spectrum of viewpoints from open acceptance to blistering condemnation. In between the two extremes, are some wonderful books that tell the stories of men and women who have left homosexual lifestyles and are experiencing a measure of healing. There are also some great books that explain what same-sex attraction is, its cause and how it can be healed. Those on the open acceptance end are intended to convince the reader that homosexuality is perfectly normal and something to be embraced and celebrated but in doing so they deceive the reader into embracing and celebrating sin. The obvious result is that the reader is bound for the eternal lake of fire if he or she does not repent and believe the gospel (see Mark 1:15 and John 3:16-20). Many of the books on blistering condemnation end of the spectrum are written by people who have very little knowledge of or experience with homosexuality and are more harm than help.

I don't apologize for the sharp tone in some sections of this book. Some will accuse me of having a chip on my shoulder or harboring some hostility toward the Church. I assure you that isn't the case. However, I do have every intention of challenging long-held beliefs and attitudes that are based on human tradition and not Biblical truth. I also intend to challenge the homosexual to see the truth of his condition.

I wrote Pure As He Is Pure to share both my struggle and what the Lord has been teaching me about how to address the various aspects of that struggle as I travel the journey toward healing and victory: particularly by becoming pure "even as He is pure" (1 John 3:3). I use myself as an example in this book because I know myself best and I didn't want to use examples of nameless, faceless, anonymous third parties. This book is mainly for the male homosexual who wants to come out of homosexuality; but I believe it will also help others who are involved with the issue: those who have homosexuals in their families and congregations, or others who want to minister to homosexuals.

To the homosexual who reads this: I've been where you are. I know what it's like to be a teenager having to hide his attraction to other boys and to keep from getting caught looking at other boys in the shower after gym. I know what it's like not to fit in because I wasn't like the other boys. I know what it's like to be called "faggot," "queer," "sissy," "homo," and other such derogatory names intended to communicate only one thing: that what you are is sick, evil, disgusting, perverted, unnatural, wrong, etc. I know what it's like to try to reconcile an attraction I didn't choose with a faith that says it's a sin for me to act on that attraction. I know what it's like to be rejected by other homosexuals because I chose to be a Christian (as the Bible defines a Christian and not as pro-gay churches define one) and rejected by other Christians because I have a same-sex attraction that I didn't choose. I know what it's like to hear those words over and over out of the mouths of Christians, "God hates you. You're sick.   You're evil.   You're an abomination. You deserve to die."

To the rest of you: I am the beneficiary of God's grace just as you are and have received His wonderful gift of salvation. It is He who has brought me out of the miry clay of homosexuality to where I am: standing on the solid Rock that is Christ. God took this solitary man and set him in that family into which we gain membership through the spirit of adoption whereby we cry Abba, Father. God brought this captive out of his captivity. God brought this rebel out of the parched desert of rebellion. God has fulfilled in me Psalm 68:6, "God setteth the solitary in families: He bringeth out those which are bound with chains: but the rebellious dwell in a dry land." It is He who has made this book possible.

Whether you're homosexual or not, I encourage you to read and study the following pages with a prayerful heart and with ears ready to hear.

that if a person is ex-gay then he or she is not only no longer involved in a homosexual lifestyle but also has gone from having same-sex attraction to having opposite-sex attraction. I don't like the term and prefer not to use it simply because of these conflicting definitions.

Gay - There was a time when this word only meant joyous and lively, merry, happy, lighthearted, or meant bright or brilliant in the sense of showy or vibrant (*gay* colors, "don we now our *gay* apparel"). However, homosexuals started using the word in reference to themselves as synonymous with the term homosexual and, so, it has come to mean a person who has same-sex attraction and/or those involved in a homosexual lifestyle. The majority of those who have come out of homosexuality use the term to mean those who are involved in a homosexual lifestyle and who embrace the political agenda of the gay rights activists. There are Christians who are rather hostile toward homosexuality and their hostility toward it invariably becomes hostility toward homosexuals - contrary to the Biblical command to love as Jesus loves. They entirely reject the term gay in connection with homosexuality. A chapter in one book on the subject says, "There's nothing gay about it." I accept the use of the term gay to refer to those homosexuals who are actively involved in and/or embracing a homosexual lifestyle and the political agenda of the gay rights activists. That is how I use the term, though sparingly, in this book.

Heterosexual (ity) - Like with the term homosexual (ity) that I will define below, there are conflicting views as to its meaning. Applying the sciences of linguistics and etymology, heterosexual can be broken down into two parts: hetero (from the Greek word heteros that is used in Jude 7), meaning other or opposite, and sexual, having to do with both gender and sexuality. In simplest terms, it means other or opposite sex. Now, here's where the conflict comes into play. Does it mean someone who has exclusively opposite-sex attraction or does it mean someone who is engaged in opposite-sex behavior? If the latter, then is a person no longer heterosexual when he or she is not engaging in sexual behavior? Is a man only heterosexual when he is actually having sex with a woman? If so, what is he when he is not having sex? I use the term to mean someone who has exclusively opposite-sex attraction or to mean something pertaining to that attraction and/or behavior.

Homosexual (ity) - Like the term heterosexual (ity) defined above, there are conflicting views as to its meaning. I've talked to many brothers and sisters in Christ who define homosexuality as "men having sex with men" and "women having sex with women." The obvious problem with that definition is with the times when a person is not actually having sex (the majority of one's life). Is a man only homosexual when he is actually having sex with another man? Most of those who are involved in ministry to those coming out of homosexuality or are themselves coming out of homosexuality (involved or participating in "ex-gay ministries"), generally define the term as behavior. They differentiate it from same-sex attraction. When they say that we are no longer homosexuals, they mean that we are no longer acting on our same-sex attraction. I use the term to mean someone who has exclusively same-sex attraction or to mean something pertaining to exclusively same-sex attraction and/or behavior.

Homosexual or Gay Lifestyle - Once called "alternative lifestyle" (implying that a person chooses this as an alternative to heterosexuality), this is another of those terms over which there tends to be considerable conflict. I, in particular, dislike this term, though I do use it in this book. So, what is it? Let's start by applying the term homosexual as commonly used by those involved in ex-gay ministries. Add to that the definition of the word lifestyle: the consistent, integrated way of life of an individual as typified by his or her manner, attitudes, possessions, etc. A homosexual or gay lifestyle (in this case homosexual and gay are interchangeable) is thus a consistent, integrated way of life that revolves around his or her same-sex attraction and acting on that attraction. It includes not merely having physical and romantic relationships with others of one's own gender but, as indicated by the definition of lifestyle, one's manner, attitudes, possessions, etc. Some homosexuals talk about gay sensibility and gay culture while denying that there is any such thing as a gay lifestyle. It seems to me that they're the same thing. In fact, lifestyle is a word that is synonymous with culture. My own objection to this term is simply in that there is not one consistent, integrated way of life by which all homosexuals can be identified. I object to the term because I find it not entirely accurate. For example, there are homosexuals who sleep around, hang out in bars and march in gay pride parades wearing nothing but a leather jock strap as they demand to be accepted in American society while attacking that society's core institutions - that's the public face of homosexuality. Other homosexuals have monogamous relationships with another person of their own gender. They go to work and to church. They don't hang out in bars or march in gay pride parades (or at least don't do so wearing next to nothing). They live quietly in your neighborhood, and their identities and lives don't revolve around their same-sex attraction. Unless you knew they were involved in a relationship with another person of their own gender, you would very likely never know that they were homosexual. In both examples, they are acting on their same-sex attraction but live very different lifestyles. If you use the term, please keep this in mind. I use the term sparingly throughout this book but place before it an indefinite article (a) instead of a definite article (the). I didn't come out of THE homosexual lifestyle, I came out of A homosexual lifestyle.

Sexual Orientation - this term is used more on the pro-homosexual side of the issue and, unfortunately, is often misconstrued by those on both sides as being synonymous with homosexual. Sexual orientation is a generic term that simply means the determinant gender object of sexual and emotional attraction. A person who has exclusively same-sex attraction has a homosexual orientation. A person who has exclusively opposite-sex attraction has a heterosexual orientation. A person who, to varying degrees, has an attraction to both sexes has a bisexual orientation (though there are many people who don't believe there is such a thing as bisexual orientation). Only the gender object of attraction determines the orientation: it has nothing to do with feelings, thoughts or behaviors.

Sexual Preference - While it is supposedly synonymous with sexual orientation, the term implies that there is a choice involved. You don't choose those to whom you are attracted. You don't wake up one morning and decide, "Oh, I think I'll start liking the opposite-sex (or same-sex) today." It is, at best, an inaccurate term.

Sin - It seems odd that I should have to define this term but my experience in dealing with people on both ends of the spectrum makes it necessary. Many Christians define sin in such a way that it also includes what many call "sinful nature." In other words, not only is behavior sin, the temptation and the inclination are sin also - at least as they apply to homosexuality. I use as my definition of sin the one Brother John used in his first epistle: "…for sin is the transgression of the law" (1 John 3:4). Law, in this case, is not restricted to the Mosaic Law. Rather, it refers to the things that God has commanded every human in every dispensation to do or not to do. Transgression is disobedience. To transgress means to disobey or to violate. As such, it is a thought or behavior and an act of the will. It is something you choose to do. Granted, humans have this unnatural bent toward sin passed on from Adam and Eve, but we choose to sin. It is not instinct and the devil didn't make us do it.

Straight - We often hear heterosexuals referred to as being "straight." The term has certain implications to it that go beyond merely identifying someone who has exclusively opposite-sex attraction. Straight suggests that one is not crooked, that one is an upstanding, law-abiding member of the community. We tell drug addicts and convicts to "get straight," in exactly this context. The Boy Scouts of America have as part of their oath being "morally straight." This doesn't mean that they are taking an oath to have opposite-sex attraction but, rather, to be upstanding, law-abiding members of the community and to behave in a morally circumspect manner. Applying the term to heterosexuality suggests that there is a moral quality to opposite-sex attraction that is not present in same-sex attraction. Since there is no choice involved, attraction is not a moral issue any more than having cancer is a moral issue. I prefer to use the terms heterosexual or opposite-sex attraction.

As I said, I insist on being rather dogmatic about these definitions. I ask that, for the time that you are spending reading this book, you use these definitions. When you come across these terms elsewhere in this book, I am using them only as defined above.

CHAPTER 2 - CAUSES

"I was born this way," the gay activist protested. "No! It's a wicked, perverted choice for which you are going to burn in the lake of fire," the conservative fundamentalist Christian retorted angrily. Who's right? Who's wrong? The activist? The fundamentalist? Both? Neither? This is what we will explore in this chapter.

When I was a little boy growing up in Niagara Falls, New York, I remember feeling like I was different from my brothers and peers. In some respects, I was different: I was more intelligent, I was emotionally sensitive, I had different interests, I was shy and introspective, and I was aesthetically inclined. Not only did I feel different, others perceived me as different. Consequently, adults tended to fawn over me while my brothers and many of my peers tended to make me the object of their cruel tauntings. Did these conspire to cause the same-sex attraction that kicked in around the time I started puberty when I was 11 years old, or to have my first crush on another boy a few years before that? We'll get to that later in the chapter. First, I want to go all the way back to the very beginning of human history: the creation and fall of humanity as told in Genesis.

GOD'S CREATED ORDER

"And the [1]LORD God said, it is not good that the man should be alone; I will make him an help meet for him" (Genesis 2:18). God's word makes it very clear that humans were never meant to be alone. From the very beginning, God saw the need for humans to form groups, starting with the most basic group: the couple. Since King James English is rather archaic, here is the same passage from the New American Standard Bible (hereafter NASB): "Then the LORD God said, it is not good for the man to be alone; I will make him a helper suitable for him." Note the last five words used in the NASB: *"a helper suitable for him"* (emphasis mine). This is God's created order: that the man should not be alone. Reading further in the second chapter of Genesis, we begin to understand the relationship that this "help meet for him" was to have with the first man. Look at Genesis 2:24, a verse quoted by Jesus in Matthew 19:5: "Therefore shall a man leave his father and his mother, and shall cleave unto his wife: and they shall be one flesh." God's created order was that the "help meet for [the man]" - the "helper suitable for him" - be the man's wife.

There is absolutely no question that God is speaking here of opposite-sex marriage and only

---

[1] In the King James, New American Standard and some other English-language Bibles, the Hebrew use of God's name - translated I AM - is rendered LORD in all capital letters. The Spanish-language Reina-Valera Bible uses Jehovah.

opposite-sex marriage. I came out of an [2]Apostolic (Oneness Pentecostal) denomination and such denominations believe that in order to establish a doctrine you have to have at least two independent passages of scripture, in context (more about context in Chapter 5), that agree with each other. We can establish the doctrine of opposite-sex marriage as God's created order by adding to Genesis 2:24 what Jesus said in Matthew 19:1-6. In that passage we read, "And it came to pass, that when Jesus had finished these sayings, He departed from Galilee, and came into the coasts of Judaea beyond Jordan: and great multitudes followed Him; and He healed them there. The Pharisees also came unto Him, tempting Him, and saying unto Him, Is it lawful for a man to put away his wife for every cause? And He answered and said unto them, Have ye not read, that He which made them at the beginning, made them male and female, and said, For this cause shall a man leave father and mother, and shall cleave to his wife; and they twain shall be one flesh? Wherefore they are no more twain, but one flesh. What therefore God hath joined together, let not man put asunder." No, there is no doubt that God's created order is opposite-sex marriage - the false

---

[2] Until coming out of homosexuality, the author was a minister in the pro-homosexual Apostolic (Oneness Pentecostal) denomination National Gay Pentecostal Alliance. Other than concerning the issues of homosexual orientation and behavior, its doctrines are nearly identical to those of the Assemblies of the Lord Jesus Christ, Pentecostal Assemblies of the World, and the United Pentecostal Church. Contrary to popular misconception, Apostolic denominations are not cults.

claims of gay theologians regarding the relationships between Ruth and Naomi, David and Jonathan and Daniel and Ashphenaz as being same-sex marriages not withstanding (more about this in Chapter 5).

THE ORIGIN OF SEXUAL ORIENTATION

The gay activist at the beginning of this chapter said, "I was born this way." We'll discuss the origin of sexual orientation within the individual later but what about the origin of sexual orientation itself? How did humans come to have this capacity to be attracted to other humans? There are a number of different answers to these questions out there but I'm going to tell you what I believe. Once again, we go back to the book of Genesis: this time to the third chapter.

In Genesis 3:16 we read, "Unto the woman He said, I will greatly multiply thy sorrow and thy conception; in sorrow thou shalt bring forth children; and thy desire shall be to thy husband, and he shall rule over thee." This is what I call "the curse." These are what God told the woman would be the consequences of her part in the first sin. There are three aspects to this "curse." I will discuss all three of them here but focus on the second one.

1. **Her sorrow and conception are multiplied** - Notice how these two go together. The Lord tells her she would not only have multiple pregnancies, but that they would not be pleasant experiences. The hormone fluctuations, the morning sickness, the intense pain just before, and during, delivery,

are all part of this. Had the transgression not taken place, I suspect there would have been fewer pregnancies and they would have been painless.

2. **Her desire would be toward her husband** - The woman would desire her husband. Now, what does that mean? The Hebrew word translated as desire is *t'shuwqah*. It is derived from *shuwq* (to run after or over as in overflow) in the original sense of stretching out after. It's meaning is that of a longing. Because of the transgression, the woman was relegated to longing after her husband. But what does this mean, both for the first woman and for the rest of humanity? That *t'shuwqah* is also used in Song of Solomon 7:10 in reference to the woman's male beloved, suggests that males also came to have this stretching out after, this longing. Thus, such desire has become a human trait experienced by both males and females. But again, what is this desire? I believe that this desire is what today we call physical and emotional attraction, the determinant gender object of which is sexual orientation. It is clear from the text that this desire is opposite-sex attraction.

3. **And he would rule over her** - This is a clear indication that, before the transgression, male and female were equals. Husband, as used here, does not have the meaning associated with husband in the sense of the agricultural husbandman and husbandry (Hebrew words *adamah* meaning soil, *ikkar* meaning farmer, and *abad* meaning to work)

or the relational (Hebrew words *baal* meaning master in its use as a modifying noun [master builder] and *chathan* meaning related by marriage). Rather, it is used - and it is the most common Old Testament use - in the sense of a companion. The Hebrew root is *iysh*, and means a man in the roles of the other and of the certain champion. The male adam's (God called them both by the generic noun adam) role was to be the female adam's other, her guaranteed champion. Hence, the common description of a spouse as being one's "other half." The Lord relegates the woman to a position where she now has a desire for her other, her champion, and where he would rule (Hebrew word *mashal* meaning to rule, have dominion, have power) over her. This position is not the position she had before the fall but praise the Lord everything will be set right when we go home to heaven.

I believe that opposite-sex attraction originated as one of the initial consequences of the first sin and that a predisposition toward it is passed on, like our unnatural bent toward sin, through the first woman's progeny much like genes are passed along. I believe that what Adam and Eve had before the fall was different but scripture doesn't explain what that is. Scripture does tell us that this desire that I call opposite-sex attraction was somehow different. So, what about same-sex attraction: is its origin also part of "the curse" in Genesis 3:16? Before we answer that, let's look at the further consequences of the first sin.

THE AFTER-EFFECTS OF THE FALL

Sin always has consequences. We're told in Ezekiel 18:20 that, "The soul that sinneth, it shall die" and in Romans 6:23, "For the wages of sin is death; but the gift of God is eternal life through Jesus Christ our Lord." However, not all of the consequences - or even most of them - are themselves sin. The ultimate consequence of sin is physical and spiritual death but we know that it is not a sin to die (for a person to be the cause of death, perhaps, but not death itself). But there were nearly infinite other consequences of sin that are not themselves sin. Do you honestly think that God created some plants to be poisonous and some animals to be venomous or carnivorous? No. These were just a couple of the after-effects of the fall, of the first sin (though the first instance of carnivores occurs after the flood). Every aspect of creation has been, in some way, corrupted or tainted by sin. Most of what we consider natural or normal are, in fact, after-effects of the fall and/or of subsequent sin. For example, the different ethnic groups, languages and skin colors are consequences of the sins of disobeying God's command to scatter throughout the planet to populate it and of trying to get God to take notice of humankind's self-sufficiency by building the tower in the place that God later called Babel (see Genesis 11).

But what about same-sex attraction? Is it's origin part of "the curse" in Genesis 3:16? While I believe that opposite-sex attraction originated there, I don't believe that's where same-sex attraction originated. So, how did we come to have same-sex attraction? I believe there was a cause for the attraction itself as a consequence of sin that I believe to be the cause of same-sex attraction in general. I also believe there are causes of same-sex attraction within the individual. The first sin brought about disease in general but there are things that also cause disease within an individual. The same is true of same-sex attraction.

THE IDOLATRY FACTOR

Perhaps one of the most misunderstood passages of scripture used in opposition to homosexuality is Romans 1:26-27. The reason it is so misunderstood is that these two verses are violently ripped from their context, thereby having the effect of bearing false witness against the word of God. I'll discuss the sin of proof texting in Chapter 4 but let's take a look at this passage in its context, which is Romans 1:18-32.

"For the wrath of God is revealed from heaven against all ungodliness and unrighteousness of men, who hold the truth in unrighteousness; Because that which may be known of God is manifest in them; for God hath shewed it unto them. For the invisible things of him from the creation of the world are clearly seen, being understood by the things that are made, even his eternal power and Godhead; so that they are without excuse: Because that, when they knew God, they glorified him not as God, neither were thankful; but became vain in their imaginations, and their foolish heart was darkened. Professing themselves to be wise, they became fools, And changed the glory of the uncorruptible God into an image made like to corruptible man, and to birds, and fourfooted beasts, and creeping things. Wherefore God also gave them up to uncleanness through the lusts of their own hearts, to dishonour their own bodies between themselves: Who changed the truth of God into a lie, and worshipped and served the creature more than the Creator, who is blessed for ever. Amen. **For this cause God gave them up unto vile affections: for even their women did change the natural use into that which is against nature: And likewise also the men, leaving the natural use of the woman, burned in their lust one toward another; men with men working that which is unseemly, and receiving in themselves that recompence of their error which was meet.** And even as they did not like to retain God in their knowledge, God gave them over to a reprobate mind, to do those things which are not convenient; Being filled with all unrighteousness, fornication, wickedness, covetousness, maliciousness; full of envy, murder, debate, deceit, malignity; whisperers, Backbiters, haters of God, despiteful, proud, boasters, inventors of evil things, disobedient to parents, Without understanding, covenantbreakers, without natural affection, implacable, unmerciful: Who knowing the judgment of God, that they which commit such things are worthy of death, not only do the same, but have pleasure in them that do them" (emphasis mine).

The key to understanding Romans 1:26-27 is in the first three words of verse 26: "***For this cause***." For what cause? For the cause that is discussed in verses 18-25: idolatry. I believe that verses 26 and 27 are part of a whole list of things that are the result of humanity abandoning God in order to serve man-made gods. We started out with the truth and then, after the fall, humanity began to "hold the truth in unrighteousness" (Romans 1:18). In holding the truth in unrighteousness we, "glorified him not as God, neither were thankful; but became vain in [our] imaginations, and [our] foolish heart was darkened." We decided that we knew better than God: "Professing [ourselves] to be wise, [we] became fools, And changed the glory of the uncorruptible God into an image made like to corruptible man, and to birds, and fourfooted beasts, and creeping things" (Romans 1:21-22).

So, where do verses 26 and 27 come in? Notice what happened next: "Wherefore God also gave [us] up to uncleanness through the lusts of [our] own hearts, to dishonour [our] own bodies between [ourselves]: Who changed the truth of God into a lie, and worshipped and served the creature more than the Creator, who is blessed for ever. Amen" (Romans 1:23-25). Because we walked away from God and started serving idols, and decided that we were wiser than God, He surrendered us to sexual impurity. Notice the connection here between idolatry and sexual impurity. We see it more clearly in other scriptures that mention temple prostitutes. God allowed us to be controlled by our own lusts. It's as if He decided, "You want to go off and worship idols? Fine. Go right ahead. You can suffer the consequences, too." Now, these consequences are not things that God brought upon us. Rather, they are the natural results of idolatry. It's like a child touching a hot burner: God doesn't burn the child's hand, the heat from the burner does. Being burned is the natural consequence of touching the hot burner. So also, sexual impurity and the list of things in the verses 23-32 are natural consequences of idolatry.

Because we (humanity) decided to go our own way and worship idols, God not only surrendered us to sexual impurity, he surrendered us to "vile affections." As an example of such affections, Brother Paul describes a phenomenon that was common in pagan fertility rites. (Yes, we're finally at verses 26 and 27). "...for even their women did change the natural use into that which is against nature: And likewise also the men, leaving the natural use of the woman, burned in their lust one toward another; men with men working that which is unseemly, and receiving in themselves that recompence of their error which was meet." I believe that this was how same-sex attraction originated: as a consequence of humanity turning its back on God in order to serve gods of its own making. Rather than being a proof text showing homosexual behavior to be sin, Romans 1:26-27 shows us how homosexual orientation (same-sex attraction) came to exist as a further result of the corrupting effects of sin upon every aspect of creation. But how does this translate into same-sex attraction within the individual?

CAUSES OF SAME-SEX ATTRACTION IN THE INDIVIDUAL

The theories on the causes of same-sex attraction in the individual abound. The conservative fundamentalist Christian at the beginning of this chapter believes that it is "a wicked, perverted choice." Others believe it is a demon - as in "the demon of homosexuality" or "the demon of lesbianism" - or at least the result of demonic influence or oppression. Still others believe it is genetic: that opposite-sex attraction and same-sex attraction are passed on from generation to generation. (The gay activist at the beginning of this chapter claimed, "I was born this way"). Finally, there are those who believe there are environmental causes - things in one's childhood - that cause a person to develop same-sex attraction that kicks in around the onset of puberty. As such, contrary to the opinion of the American Psychological Association, it is a mental disorder or a neurosis (for more information about same-sex attraction in this context, go to the website for the National Association for Research and Therapy of Homosexuality listed in the Resources section at the end of this book). So, how does a person come to have same-sex attraction?

This is where it becomes necessary to examine the lives of those who have same-sex attraction, whether they are living a homosexual lifestyle or are struggling to overcome same-sex attraction. While scientists are conducting genetic studies with dubious results that are, at best, inconclusive, very few researchers are studying environmental causes. Those who are conducting such research are often dismissed by the secular science community as homophobic, anti-homosexual hatemongers. I visited the website of one organization that focuses on the psychological treatment methodology known as reparative therapy. That site listed a number of environmental factors seen as risk factors in causing same-sex attraction in boys. Many of the national ex-gay ministries seem to have adopted the same view regarding these factors. My conversations with other "ex-gay" men suggest that these risk factors are valid. I also took those factors and looked at the place each of them had in my own childhood. I added two characteristics that I had come across elsewhere: intelligence and creativity. I use my own life as an example because I know that life best and one of the purposes of this book is to share my own struggle with homosexuality. Here are those factors and their role in my childhood.

SENSITIVE TEMPERAMENT - I was an emotionally sensitive child. From as far back as I can remember, I had been known as a child who was what many adults called "tender hearted." I was a gentle child. I laughed and cried easily. I was, in fact, what some might have called a "crybaby;" though there was more to it than that. Such a temperament, though, was eventually suppressed deep inside as I had to protect my fragile emotions from being smashed into the ground as they frequently were by those in my life who seemed to feel it their duty to pick on me: older half-brothers, mom's boyfriends, and less-intelligent peers. By the time I was a teen, I had become a very cold, unfeeling person. It took until I was in an opposite-sex marriage for almost five years for me to restore my ability to have more than the most superficial of emotions (I entered that marriage primarily for that purpose).

AESTEHETICALLY INCLINED - I remember when I was a little boy a habit developed that I carried with me into adulthood. I was never good at any of the various arts other than being able to write well, and was often envious of those who, like my dad, could play the guitar. But whenever I walked into a home or other building, I was automatically redesigning it in my head, imagining how I would do things differently. It wasn't something I paid much attention to, or even that I often realized was happening, but it was there nonetheless. I still find myself doing it even today. I live in the historic Linwood District of Buffalo, New York and one side of my apartment building is on Linwood Avenue. All along that street there are just the most beautiful Victorian-era homes and I find myself feeling a certain awe and excitement just walking past some of those homes on my way to church or, when the weather is nice, to work.

PREFERRED ACTIVITIES - No, I didn't like sports. I was never any good at athletic activity. I was the kid who was picked for teams in gym class only because I was the last person left. My relationship with sports was like that of oil and water: sports and I just didn't go together. In my early teens I once saw an outdoor soccer game on television and, for the first time, I found a sport that I actually liked. That doesn't mean that I ever really learned how to play. After all, I grew up in a part of the country where, and in an era when, soccer had not caught on (in the days before the advent of the soccer mom). When I was in the Navy, stationed on my first ship, a Marine Corps friend of mine and I would often go to a park out in town - my homeport of Yokosuka, Japan - and play soccer with some of the local kids. About a year before I left the Navy in 1992, some guys from my last ship and I were at my El Cajon, California apartment one evening and we were outside kicking a soccer ball around. I tore the meniscus in my left knee and found myself having to permanently give up playing soccer. Today, I have to settle for following soccer scores on the Internet or watching videos of prior World Cup matches to get my soccer fix. As for other activities, I had my big metal Tonka trucks that I liked to play with (that was back in the days when such toys were still made of genuine American steel instead of plastic), as well as toy guns that looked very realistic; but I preferred activities that required intelligence and intuition than playing traditionally "boy" games. While there was a group of boys with whom I often hung around, I spent a lot of time talking with the girls.

PORNOGRAPHY - Late on Friday nights while mom was out at the bars, my older brothers and I would watch pornographic movies on a Canadian television station (Niagara Falls, New York is on the American side of the border with Canada and we could get some of the television stations from Hamilton and Toronto). My older brothers, already in their early teens, were focusing on the women but I, secretly, was focused on the men and their penises - often wishing the women would just go away.

SEXUAL ABUSE - I don't know if I can honestly say I was sexually abused. I remember when I was boy, definitely before I was eight or nine, standing on one side of a garage next door where there were a lot of small trees and other plant life in the space between the garage and the fence to the next yard, a space less than four feet wide. Anyway, I was there with this Tuscarora kid about my age, maybe a little older I don't remember. One time we were back there and he talked me into performing oral sex on him. Then there was a time I was at the house of my best friend, a kid who was maybe three or four years older than I who was into collecting insects, caring for injured birds, and keeping fish tanks of tropical fish. One day, his next younger brother (but still older than I by at least two years) and I were in one of the bedrooms and he had me try to perform anal sex on him. Finally, there was a time when I was in Boy Scouts (yes, I was in scouting for about three years or so until I was 11) and I went down the street to where one of the other boys in my troop lived. We were in his room and he convinced me to perform oral sex on him (convincing me didn't take much effort on his part, though). In all of these situations, no one had ever forced me to do anything: while I didn't initiate these encounters, I was a very willing participant. That's why I can't really say I was abused because I did those things willingly and was fully cognizant of what I was doing. It would be more accurate to call it sexual experimentation.

ABSENT/PASSIVE FATHER, DOMINEERING MOTHER - My family environment was definitely not the norm, particularly in the era in which I grew up (the 1960s and 1970s). My mom was a single mom on welfare who had five kids from three different guys. My dad, who was never married to my mom, fathered 17 kids from his two marriages and at least three other relationships. I was the only one of his kids that my mom bore. So, I was - to use an archaic phrase - a bastard child in a household of bastard children (my mom was never married to any of the men who fathered her children). I knew who my dad was. Of all his kids, at least five of which were boys, I was the one who was named after him (though another of his sons has the same first name). We even did things together on occasion, though often that meant my being at his house or hanging out in bars with him. As for my biological mom, I don't know how anyone could say she was domineering because, quite honestly, she was very rarely ever home. Most of her various boyfriends, some of whom lived with us, were home more often than she was. The five of us kids were essentially left to fend for ourselves.

LACK OF AFFECTION/AFFIRMATION FROM ONE'S SAME-GENDER PARENT - That a child didn't receive adequate love and attention from the parent of that child's gender seems to be a primary cause of same-sex attraction. Well, I must admit that I could never get close to my dad emotionally but much of that was because I didn't get emotionally close to anyone, though much of it was his inability or unwillingness to develop any kind of relationship with me. One thing in particular sticks out in my mind, though: whenever we were together, he would alternately claim to be my father but would also tell me that someone else was my father. Further, there was never any affection shown in my family, whether from my father, whom I only saw on occasion, or from my mother who was generally not home anyway. Not once were words like, "I love you" ever exchanged. Not once was a hug of comfort or affection ever given, at least not since any time that I can remember (going back to about age four).

PICKED ON OR TEASED BY PEERS FOR BEING PERCEIVED AS DIFFERENT - I was often picked on or teased as a boy; whether by my older brothers, my peers or even by some adults, I was an easy target. Being emotionally sensitive, I cried easily as my feelings were often smashed into the ground. I was picked on or teased because I was different from other boys. I was smarter than they were. I was emotionally sensitive. I liked activities that involved using my brain. I didn't like sports or very many outdoor games though I did play kick ball or hide and seek with my siblings and friends and spent a lot of time playing down in the Niagara gorge or with my realistic-looking toy guns or my Tonka trucks. I was different in other ways too. I was late in learning things like riding a bicycle or tying my shoes - I think I was around nine years old when I finally learned. I didn't like to fight and, in fact, was rather afraid to do so. I remember one time when I was nine that my older brothers and sister took me over onto the next block and made me fight this other boy my age that had been giving me a hard time. There was another time, however, when I was the same age, when my best friend's youngest brother (who was my age) got me in trouble with the police because I was seen with him later in the day after he had stolen five dollars from a woman's car. Because I was embarrassed to tell the police that I was hanging out in the Manpower office where this woman who worked there had befriended me ever since I was around six, I was charged as an accessory. Ever since then, until my mom died when I was 11, I would beat him up every time I saw him. And, at one point, I even burned down his family's garage.

I admit that I was different in many ways. Even my sleeping arrangements were different. My peers all either had their own bedrooms or shared them with another male sibling. My two older brothers, younger brother, and mentally retarded uncle (who lived with us) shared a room. My "room" was a full-sized box spring and mattress in a wide section of the upstairs hall between the wall outside my brothers' room and the railing above the stairs. It was just wide enough for that box spring and mattress and the railing was long enough to where I had that and a chest of drawers where my clothes were kept. At the head of the box spring and mattress in that section of the hall was a window that overlooked the used car lot next door that, when I was around 10, became the parking lot for Off-Track Betting. One final way in which I was different was in the object of my first crush. Many boys some time before puberty have a crush on some girl. My first crush was on another boy in the neighborhood, part of the group of boys with which I hung around. His name was Tim. He was this angelic-looking boy who, like me, had blond hair and blue eyes. He was my age but a bit shorter than the rest of us. He was also missing the fingers on his right hand just above the second knuckle, so they were little stubs that had no function. We weren't very good friends but, to me, he was the most beautiful person I had ever seen and I had certain feelings for him that I can't fully explain. Of course, I could never let on that I thought of him that way because the worst thing to be called in that neighborhood was "queer" and I didn't want to risk that. So, I ended up having to admire him from afar.

INTELLIGENCE AND CREATIVITY - Some people say that homosexuals are often more intelligent and/or creative than heterosexuals. I don't know how true that is but as a percentage of their respective populations, homosexuals do tend to possess greater intelligence and creativity. The gay community likes to point to all the well-known creative geniuses that were supposedly homosexual, such as Michelangelo,

Shakespeare and Tchaikovsky. Well, of the five of us kids in my biological family, I was the smart one. I was the one who got well above average grades in school without even trying - particularly in the subjects of reading, language arts and social studies. Unfortunately, because I did so well in school without any effort, I was left to fend for myself: no one ever pushed me to make any kind of effort. I understood things as a child that we often think children couldn't possibly understand, and I paid attention as I watched the news or - as I very often liked to watch - talk shows. As a means of escaping a lot of the hurt I endured as a child, I tended to withdraw into my brain and think and analyze and imagine. Whenever I read a book, I was able to place myself right into the story and just get lost there. As an adult in the mid-1980s I qualified for and joined Mensa, the society for people with IQs in the top two percent of the population. I'm not sure there is a cause and effect relationship between these and same-sex attraction but the circumstantial evidence makes it more than coincidence.

Those are the risk factors that, except for intelligence and creativity, ex-gay ministries often assert to be causes of homosexuality in boys. We acquired same-sex attraction because of those things though there may also be a biological component (a predisposition toward same-sex attraction). I've been in contact with a number of men who, as I do, struggle with same-sex attraction. I've also read numerous testimonies of men who have come out of a homosexual lifestyle. All of them have experienced at least some of the risk factors mentioned above - especially the lack of love and affection from their dads. I accept the aforementioned factors as being at least influential in causing same-sex attraction. Admittedly, not every boy who was raised in such an environment as mine or had similar characteristics as the ones discussed above became homosexual. This does not mean that such things don't cause same-sex attraction in males. Why didn't my two older brothers and younger brother become homosexual? They didn't have fathers at home (and, in fact, had less contact with their fathers than I had with mine). Our mom was never home for them. They never received affection or attention from the parent of their own gender. My older brothers watched the same pornography that I watched (it was with them that I watched it).

I intentionally have not discussed same-sex attraction in girls because there is a different dynamic involved that I don't understand though sexual abuse and a lack of affection/affirmation from their mothers are often believed to be major factors. Information on how same-sex attraction is caused in girls is available from Exodus and other sources.

Before we move on, it's important for me to continue my story beyond my early childhood. I started puberty when I was 11. My mom died over that summer between sixth grade and my first year of junior high school and I went to live with my dad's oldest living daughter, Muriel (his first daughter died in a motorcycle accident on her 22nd birthday in 1972). She and I didn't get along too well. Before letting me spend any more time with my best friend (the one who was into collecting insects, caring for injured animals and keeping tropical fish), she insisted on meeting him as any good parent would. As I said, he was three or four years older than I. He came over to the apartment where we were living and sat in the living room on the couch. He was rather unkempt in appearance, somewhat dark-skinned (his parents came to the United States from Greece before he was born), and sat rather effeminately. I was allowed to escort him back to his house but was to return immediately afterward. The tension as I walked in the door was so thick you could cut it with a knife. Muriel was furious. She told me I was never to see him again because he was "queer." I knew well what the word meant but, in his defense, there wasn't a sexual bone in his body. Not only was he not interested in other boys, he wasn't interested in girls either. He had no sexual interests whatsoever. When she told my dad about him one day on the phone (he was living in Florida where he worked as a truck driver), he talked to me and asked me things like whether my friend liked to engage in oral sex (he used a much more colorful phrase), to which I told him the truth and said that he had no such interests. What I didn't tell him or anyone else was that I was starting to have such interests in boys, though not in that particular boy.

It was a difficult few months for Muriel and me and in early October 1975, it all came to a head. We got into this heated argument, well heated on her end because when I was being yelled at I tended to clam up. I told her that I didn't want to live with her anymore. It only took one phone call and, about an hour afterward, I was on my way to go live with my dad's cousin, Avon, who had adopted his oldest daughter's son after she died in that motorcycle accident three years earlier. (Avon later adopted me and, while neither of us were known for being very affectionate, I think I would have ended up going down a very different road - drugs, crime, etc. - if she hadn't provided the structure and discipline that I needed but hadn't received before then). Living with Avon was a real culture shock. She lived in a middle-class neighborhood. All of a sudden, I had rules to follow, chores to do, and other things that were more like normal. I even had my own bedroom most of the time. It took a while for me to adjust and I had subconsciously decided that the best way for me to get through this was to simply keep my mouth shut and do what I was told. I started at a new school, which was rather traumatic for me because these people were so different from the kinds of kids I was used to being around. (I started junior high school in the school I would have gone to if my mom were still alive: a school that had a reputation for being the toughest school in town; a place where the bad kids went to school). But the hardest part was taking showers with the other boys after gym or swim class. I found myself becoming sexually aroused by the nakedness of some of the other boys, but managed to keep myself from getting an erection. When I got home, I would fantasize about what I wanted to do with some of those boys and then I would masturbate. I received salvation when I was 13, in December 1976, while watching The 700 Club but that didn't take away what I was feeling about other boys.   I had heard in church how homosexuality was evil and I pleaded with the Lord to take away my homosexual thoughts (I wasn't ready to admit to myself that I was homosexual but I had exclusively homosexual thoughts).   This was around the time when Anita Bryant was engaged in her activism against homosexuality.

This secret struggle continued through high school and afterward when I joined the Navy. I tried so hard to fight my homosexual attractions. I had never acted on them since before puberty other than inside my very active brain. When I was 19 and had been in the Navy for more than a year, I fell into sexual sin by having my first sexual experience. It was an act of defiance in an attempt to prove to the guys on my first ship - who had been calling me names like "faggot" and "queer" - that I wasn't that way.   We were in port in the Philippines and one night after leaving the Christian Servicemen's Center, I went out onto the main drag where nearly every sailor in port hung out in the various bars.   I went into one of the bars and eventually had one of the hostesses (a euphemism for women who would have sex with you if you paid the manager a fine for the loss of her services) take me home with her. I made sure some of the guys on my ship saw me with her by walking up the street past some of the open-air bars where they were. It had the desired effect as they cheered me on. This woman took me to her house and, going on memory from those pornographic movies I saw as a young boy, I had sex with her. Since then, I started walking away from the Lord.   Not long afterward, I had become the stereotypical heterosexual drunken sailor and had sex with women in nearly every port. I had even subscribed to Playboy magazine when I was on one ship. Yet, none of this changed the fact that I was sexually and emotionally attracted only to other males. I masturbated regularly, fantasizing about some of the guys that I would see naked in the shower or in the berthing compartment. It was a lot of work to not get caught looking at other guys.

My first sexual experience with a man was when I was 22. I was stationed with a destroyer squadron staff in San Diego, California and had gone to a gay bar out of curiosity. I allowed this guy from Tijuana, Mexico come onto me and pick me up. We then went to a motel and had sex. Unlike all the sex I'd had with women, this felt natural, normal, right (one of the deceptions of homosexuality is that it feels as if it's natural for us to be attracted to the same gender and to engage in sexual activity with others of our own gender). Yet, I didn't pursue anything with that or any other man after that night except for trying to come on to this one heterosexual friend of mine one weekend a little over a year later - I got as far as being allowed to give him a massage as he lay on the floor in his briefs. I continued to have my secret fantasies and still masturbated as an almost nightly ritual.

A couple of months after my first sexual experience with a man, I went home on leave. Avon's oldest daughter, Dollie (who was already grown and married when I went to live there) had a best friend who had stopped by her house one night. We met, started talking and - after I went back to California where I was then stationed on a helicopter carrier and, later, on staff at Naval Training Center San Diego - we wrote to each other. We carried on a relationship mainly by mail but whenever I got home on leave, we'd get together to go on dates and, sometimes, have sex. Almost two years later we were talking on the phone long distance. There was something about this woman that drew me to her. I wasn't attracted to her sexually or emotionally but she had a quality that I felt I was missing in my life. She was very open and free with her emotions and was able to express them spontaneously. I had long lost my ability to feel more than the most superficial of emotions and I wanted to get that back. I don't know why or what brought it about, but she and I were talking on the phone one night in early 1987 (I was in San Diego, California and she was in Niagara Falls, New York). During the conversation, I said rather casually, "Well, we could always just get married." We got engaged that night over the phone and, a year later, were married. I figured that if I plunged right into the most intimate of human relationships, I would learn how to regain the ability to feel and even learn to love her. Part of me was also thinking that maybe this would "cure" me of my same-sex attraction. We were married for almost five years and they were the most emotionally traumatic years of my life. I learned how to feel emotions again, but it had been a very painful process for both of us. Dollie and my adoptive mom tried to warn me before we even got engaged that she was a very controlling and domineering woman. Dollie also tried to warn her that I was essentially incapable of real emotion (but my now ex-wife vowed that she would change me). Being in that marriage taught me how to have emotions again; but as I let myself feel, I was losing the control for which I was all-too-well known. The marriage lasted as long as it did only because I was still in the Navy for most of it and could get away for a day (24-hour duty on board ship once every three, four, five or six days depending on the duty rotation), week, month, or six months at a time depending on my ship's schedule. I generally resisted having sex with her because of her nature and mainly because I just didn't feel that way about her. But, in 1990, she became pregnant with our daughter, Amanda. That was another frightening experience as I now faced the prospect of being a father. We stuck it out and, in 1992, I took advantage of the Navy's downsizing to get out of the Navy and take my family back home to Western New York State. One of the nice things about being in the Navy was being able to get away from her for a while. I no longer had that and it soon took its toll. It got to the point where I felt I was losing my ability to control the anger and hostility I was feeling toward her. Afraid that I would become violent, one morning in November 1992 I left her a note I had written the night before, packed some things into my car and left her and our daughter. I filed for divorce within days after that, a painful process that took almost a year.

During the process of the divorce, I got counseling to deal with my emotions and my inability to control them. The counseling went well and I learned to have healthy emotions and express them appropriately.

During that time, independent of the counseling, I made a conscious decision to remove all the façades I had built up around me and become my genuine self, whatever that was. That led me to, for the first time, say to myself those three little words: "I am gay." As we were in the process of negotiating visitation with my daughter through a mediator, I revealed my same-sex attraction to my now ex-wife. She wasn't happy with it but we managed to work around it. A few months later, I learned about a gay support group that met monthly and went to a meeting. It was there that I learned about the gay bars in Buffalo (I lived in Niagara Falls). I started going down there and soon started having sex with different men. I quickly got to the point where I was rather promiscuous. I had also become somewhat of a gay activist as I more openly acknowledged my homosexual orientation.

In 1995, I had learned about a gay Pentecostal denomination, the National Gay Pentecostal Alliance, as I was reading a secular book about being gay. I contacted that denomination's presbyter and, after correspondence over a few months, I returned to faith in Jesus as I repented for all my years of abandoning Him. I stopped going to the bars and having sex with other men (except for a few times when I fell). I had also told the Lord that He could do whatever He wanted with my homosexual orientation, and continued to tell him that from time to time in the years since, making the old hymn I Surrender All my prayer. The following year, after completing the National Gay Pentecostal Alliance's Bible school requirements, I was ordained and started a church in Niagara Falls.

Almost three years later, the Lord had me close the church to pursue prophetic and teaching ministry. (Contrary to popular misconception, there are men and women with same-sex attraction who are genuinely saved and filled with the Holy Ghost. If they are living a homosexual lifestyle as I was, or are otherwise embracing their same-sex attraction, then they are simply in rebellion just as anyone who has a besetting sin that he or she chooses not to lay aside). Finally, in late August 2001, I began looking at the claims of ex-gay ministries and asked the Lord to show me the truth about their claims. The Lord showed me some other things in my life that I had to deal with as well. Specifically, I was in bondage to masturbation and what I call mental lechery (extreme sexual promiscuity occurring in the mind). I had also become what Psalm 68:6 calls solitary but was resisting the Lord's attempts to correct that. He has rewarded me by reducing the frequency and intensity of my looking at other guys to lust after them, as well as the frequency with which I masturbated (which had become a nightly ritual). Since then, the Lord has given me the victory over both the masturbation and the extreme lusts.

CHAPTER 3 - CHOICES

Just as there are causes, so also there are choices. The gay community argues that they didn't choose their same-sex attraction, that they were born that way and, so, it is only right for them to act on that attraction. Failure to act on that attraction by pursuing homosexual sex and relationships, they argue, is to deny who you are as a person. They argue that if you're not embracing your same-sex attraction and acting on that attraction through homosexual sex and relationships, you're repressing your sexuality, you're not being true to yourself, and you're living a lie. If we adhere to that logic then, since we were all born with an unnatural bent toward sin (a "sinful nature") passed on from Adam and Eve, we should act on that unnatural bent by engaging in sin. After all, we didn't choose to desire sin so why not act on our sinful nature? Brother Paul answers this in Romans 6:1-7,

"What shall we say then? Shall we continue in sin, that grace may abound? God forbid. How shall we, that are dead to sin, live any longer therein? Know ye not, that so many of us as were baptized into Jesus Christ were baptized into his death? Therefore we are buried with him by baptism into death: that like as Christ was raised up from the dead by the glory of the Father, even so we also should walk in newness of life. For if we have been planted together in the likeness of his death, we shall be also in the likeness of his resurrection: Knowing this, that our old man is crucified with him, that the body of sin might be destroyed, that henceforth we should not serve sin. For he that is dead is freed from sin."

Scripture is abundantly clear in stating that we are **not** to act on our unnatural bent toward sin, our "sinful nature." Rather, we are to obey the commands of God and not sin. Ezekiel tells us in Ezekiel 18:20, "The soul that sinneth, it shall die. The son shall not bear the iniquity of the father, neither shall the father bear the iniquity of the son: the righteousness of the righteous shall be upon him, and the wickedness of the wicked shall be upon him." We're told in John 5:14, "Afterward Jesus findeth him in the temple, and said unto him, Behold, thou art made whole: sin no more, lest a worse thing come unto thee." In John 8:11 we read, "She said, No man, Lord. And Jesus said unto her, Neither do I condemn thee: go, and sin no more." Paul tells us in Romans 6:23, "For the wages of sin is death; but the gift of God is eternal life through Jesus Christ our Lord." These are by no means all of the scriptures that tell us not to sin or tell us the consequences of sinning but they clearly state that we are not to sin.

The argument that because we didn't choose to have same-sex attraction we have unlimited license to embrace that attraction and engage in homosexual sin, is a faulty one. It has been suggested that some people have a genetic predisposition toward alcoholism. Does that mean those people have a license to pick up that first drink? It has been suggested that child abuse is passed on from generation to generation, meaning that if dad did it, you're likely to do it too. Does that give you license to abuse your child? No, no, no: a thousand times, no! We are responsible for our own actions. Same-sex attraction is not natural. It is not normal. God didn't create anyone to have same-sex attraction. Contrary to the opinion of the American Psychiatric Association, it is a mental illness, a neurosis. It isn't something to be embraced and celebrated, it's something to be treated and healed. So, when and what did I choose?

WHEN AND WHAT DID I CHOOSE?

The conservative fundamentalist Christian at the beginning of Chapter 2 would tell me that my same-sex attraction is a wicked, perverted choice for which I'm going to burn in the lake of fire. Having actually been told that, my question is this: "When and what did I choose?"

Only those who have no real experience with and knowledge of homosexuality will affirmatively state that same-sex attraction is a choice. Even opposite-sex attraction came about not as a choice but as a direct consequence of the first sin (it is the "desire" in Genesis 3:16). Yet, we who have same-sex attraction did make choices. Here's an article that I came across in the website of Eagle's Wings Ministry, a resource that has been very helpful to me in understanding some of the issues around getting victory over same-sex attraction. The article is titled Homosexual

Discoveries And Choices[f]. The article's discussion of differentness is something to which I can particularly relate.

"Most people who have 'come out of the closet' and declared themselves to be homosexual believe that they were born that way and therefore can do nothing about it. Indeed, it seems to be a plausible explanation, since many testify that they have felt "different" from a very early age. The reasonable thing to do, it is argued, is to accept what cannot be changed and live it out. Much time and energy has been spent by the homosexual community to promote this belief in society and the church with astonishing results.

"The only problem with the theory is that there is no generally accepted scientific evidence at present to support it, although such evidence has been diligently sought. Dr. William Wilson, former head of the Division of Biological Psychiatry at Duke University, has closely followed the research that has been done to try to prove this theory. He concludes, 'There is no evidence that genetic or hormonal factors play any role in the development of homosexuality' (Answers to Your Questions About Homosexuality, edited by C. Lanning, p. 156). Dr. Edmund Bergler in Homosexuality: Disease or Way of Life, New York: Collier

---

[f] Used by permission.

Books, 1962, p. 166 states, 'The color of a person's eyes cannot be changed therapeutically, but homosexuality can be changed by psychotherapy.'

"Furthermore, homosexuals assert that to ask them to change is not only unkind, but impossible. Indeed many have experienced intense struggle with their sexual preferences, and have tried to deny them, repent of them (which is no more reasonable than for a heterosexually oriented person to repent of being attracted to the opposite sex) and plead with God to take away the feelings - all to no avail. The only choice left it seems is to accept the orientation and live the lifestyle. None of the above efforts involve doing the things that do result in orientation change - namely, understanding and dealing with the root causes as is done in psycho/spiritual therapy. Dr. Reuben Fine stated, 'I have recently had occasion to review the results of psychotherapy with homosexuals, and been surprised by the findings. It is paradoxical that even though the politically active homosexual group denies the possibility of change, all studies from Schrenck-Notzing on have found positive effects...If the patients were motivated, whatever procedure is adopted, a large percentage will give up their homosexuality. In this connection public information is of the greatest importance. The misinformation spread by certain circles that "homosexuality is untreatable by psychotherapy" does incalculable harm to thousands of men and women' [Reuben Fine, "Psychoanalytic Theory, Male and Female Homosexuality: Psychological Approaches" edited by Louis Diamant, (Washington, D.C., Hemisphere Publishing Corporation, 1987), p. 84-86].

"It is true that the homosexually orientated person did not choose this orientation. This was something which was discovered over the course of the growing up process. It is also true, however, that what is done with the orientation is the choice of the person. Eagles' Wings desires to offer homosexuals the choice of exploring the origins of the homosexual desires, dealing with the underlying psychological condition, receiving inner healing for the hurts of the past, and developing a secure gender identity. This is done within the context of trusting that God is on the side of the person, with him/her in the process, not waiting until change has occurred to give love and acceptance. God will give the motivation and power to persevere in the healing process. Individual counseling and group support are tools He often uses in this journey toward wholeness."

So, when and what did I choose? Looking back at my childhood, I know that I didn't choose to have same-sex attraction. I didn't choose most of the various factors that certainly contributed to if not caused my same-sex attraction. I did choose to **act** on that attraction. It is true, regardless of what many well-meaning folks say about children not being capable of making such choices, that I chose to participate in those few incidents of sexual experimentation with other boys. I also chose to watch pornography with my older half-brothers. I chose to lust after other guys when I should have been "bringing into captivity every thought to the obedience of Christ" (2 Corinthians 10:5). I mentioned earlier my sexual experiences that occurred before puberty and said that I was a willing participant. I chose, when I was in my early 20s, to have that first sexual experience with another man. After I left my marriage, I chose to embrace my same-sex attraction and to be sexually promiscuous with other men. I chose to live a homosexual lifestyle. And, finally, I chose to pursue the path toward healing my same-sex attraction and toward gaining victory over homosexual sin. It is over this whole issue of causes and choices that the debate about the "sin of homosexuality" rages. For more information about causes and choices, I encourage you to obtain the video Understanding Homosexuality: Roots And Recovery. This video is one of the sessions of the 1995 Exodus Conference and is taught by Sy Rogers a former transsexual whom the Lord has mercifully healed. It is available as part of Exodus International's Foundational Issues Series. You can purchase a copy through Exodus.

We must accept responsibility for the choices we make in our lives regardless of anything that happened to us. Even though the desire to sin was passed on to us through Adam and Eve, we're still responsible for the sins we commit. So also, even though there were things in our childhoods that caused us to develop same-sex attraction we're responsible for having chosen to act on that attraction by engaging in homosexual thoughts and behaviors. In the next chapter we'll discuss the sin of homosexuality.

CHAPTER 4 - THE SIN OF HOMOSEXUALITY

We discussed in Chapter 1 the definition of sin because of this chapter. There is much confusion it seems as to what sin itself is and what things are sinful. This is why accurate definitions are so important. I've heard brothers and sisters in Christ say that sin is not limited to things that you think or do but also includes a person's nature. In the context of homosexuality, I think many of them use a broader, unbiblical definition of sin so that they can justify calling same-sex attraction sinful. In their hatred of homosexual behavior, they want to make sure that they don't appear to in any way even remotely support anything having to do with homosexuality. In their minds, to acknowledge as we have here that same-sex attraction is not a choice is the same as supporting the sin of homosexuality. As those of us who are being healed of our same-sex attraction, and who have left homosexual lifestyles can tell you, this couldn't be further from the truth. So, we're going to sort the things that are sin from the things that aren't.

WHAT IS SIN?

Let's go back to our definition of sin. In Chapter 1, I said that I use as my definition of sin the one Brother John used in his first epistle: "...for sin is the transgression of the law" (1 John 3:4). Law, in this case, is not restricted to the Mosaic Law (a topic I will discuss in Chapter 5) but, rather, refers to the things that God has commanded every human in every dispensation to do or not to do. Transgression is disobedience. To transgress means to disobey, to violate. As such, it is a thought or behavior and an act of the will. It is something you choose to do. Granted, humans have this [3]unnatural bent toward sin passed on from Adam and Eve, but we choose to sin. It is not instinct and the devil didn't make us do it. Sin is always a choice, always an act of the will. Our unnatural bent toward sin not withstanding, we are not forced to sin. One of the most heretical and faithless statements that Christians often make about sin is that "We will sin." By making that statement, they've already surrendered to our enemies (the world, the flesh and Satan). A righteous God doesn't tell us to "Go and sin no more" (John 5:14 and 8:11) if He believes that we are incapable of obeying Him. Granted, we need His help and His strength to obey but we can obey. He who said, "Go and sin no more" is He who "will with the temptation [to sin] also make a way to escape, that ye may be able to bear it" (1 Corinthians 10:13) and is He "that is able to keep you from falling, and present you faultless before the presence of His glory with exceeding joy" (Jude 24). We are not powerless against sin as Christians because

---

[3] The author acknowledges that scripture calls this the "sinful nature" but believes that there is nothing "natural" after the first sin in the Garden of Eden (the fall) because all of creation has been corrupted or otherwise damaged by sin. Essentially, the author believes that it is unnatural for humans to sin but because of the fall we want to sin.

He who is all-powerful dwells within us. As Brother Paul wrote to the church at Philippi: "I can do all things through Christ which strengtheneth me" (Philippians 4:13). While Brother Paul was specifically referring to abounding and suffering need, the principle also applies to overcoming sin. If we were automatically going to sin and had no hope of avoiding it, then King David could not say as he did in Psalm 119:11, "Thy word have I hid in mine heart, ***that I might not sin against Thee***" (emphasis mine).

One of the most evil statements to ever come out of the mouths or pens of Christians is one that was a popular bumper sticker in the late 1970s and early 1980s. No other statement has so fully communicated the message that we Christians have surrendered to our enemies. That statement is, "Christians aren't perfect, just forgiven." By that statement, we have thrown down our swords and our armor. By that statement, we willingly put ourselves back under sin's tyrannical control. It excuses lives of carnality and worldliness. It is the very reason that we "have not yet resisted unto blood, striving against sin" (Hebrews 12:4). No wonder so many Christians say and believe that "we WILL sin!" and thereby display a belief in such damnable heresies as one in which we have given up on the victory that is in Jesus (the author pauses to sing the old hymn, Victory In Jesus).

Yet, that is not what God's word tells us. God's word tells us that we are no longer slaves to sin but, rather, slaves to God (see Romans 6:16-18). If we are no longer slaves to sin we can't be forced to sin. **We**

can choose not to sin! "For sin ***shall not*** have dominion over you…" (Romans 6:14; emphasis mine).

So, what is sin? Sin is any thought or behavior by which we disobey the commands of God. As such, it is a choice and act of the will. It is rebellion against God. It is when a person "looketh on a woman to lust after her" (Matthew 5:28). It is when we are drawn away by our own lusts and are enticed. It is also what is brought forth when our lust has conceived (see James 1:13-15). In specific regard to homosexuality, it is our looking at another person of our own gender to lust after him. It is also when our lusting after another person of our own gender has conceived and we start playing out scenarios in the mind of having sex with that person or we actually engage in sexual activity with that person, or when we pursue sexual/romantic relationships with others of our own gender that are contrary to God's created design.

Attraction is not sin. That you happen to pass by someone in the produce aisle at the supermarket and are drawn to specific physical features (the first thing I notice is a person's eyes) or you meet someone and are romantically drawn to non-physical characteristics is not sin. Now, if you decide to act on that attraction by thinking about how you'd like to see that person naked or would like to have sex with that person or you start letting yourself get romantically attached to this person, that is sin because you've gone beyond attraction and allowed yourself to lust, entertain impure thoughts or, in the case of the emotional attraction, allowed yourself to relate in a way to another of your own gender that is contrary to God's created design.

Attraction is also not temptation. Many who struggle with same-sex attraction make the mistake of calling that attraction temptation. Merely being attracted to others of your own gender or the opposite gender doesn't mean you're tempted to have sex with that person. However, if you dwell on the attraction and allow yourself to entertain thoughts about that attraction, then it will lead to temptation (though it will not lead to dancing).

Temptation is not sin. It is merely the enticement to sin. If temptation were itself sin, then the scripture would be a contradictory lie which says about our beloved Lord Jesus, "…but was in all points tempted like as we are, yet without sin" (Hebrews 4:15). Further, if temptation were sin, how then would Jesus use it to help us keep from sinning? As Brother Paul said in 1 Corinthians 10:13, "There hath no temptation taken you but such as is common to man: but God is faithful, Who will not suffer you to be tempted above that ye are able; but will **with the temptation** also make a way to escape, that ye may be able to bear it" (emphasis mine).

It is quite clear that sin has a very specific definition as those thoughts or behaviors by which we disobey the commands of God. So, then, what is the sin of homosexuality?

THE SIN OF HOMOSEXUALITY

We had to clearly define sin itself before we could define the sin of homosexuality. Is there even a separate sin of homosexuality; or is homosexuality simply a form of various sexual sins such as adultery, fornication, pornography, rape, molestation, incest, promiscuity, prostitution, etc.? That men having sex with men is clearly identified as a separate sin in Leviticus 18:22 and 20:13 suggests that there is a separate sin of homosexuality; or is it simply homosexual fornication? Deuteronomy 23:17 identifies [4]same-sex male prostitution and, so, that indicates that there is a homosexual form of prostitution. The men of Gibeah, in Judges 19:22-25 wanted to rape the old man's male Levite guest, indicating a homosexual form of rape.

So, is there or is there not a separate sin of homosexuality? Yes. In Chapter 2 we briefly discussed God's created order for sexual expression as being between a man and a woman in the context of marriage. Inasmuch as homosexuality is contrary to that created order, there is a separate sin of homosexuality. However, the scriptures cited above mention the sins of fornication, prostitution and rape where both parties just happened to be of the same gender. So, in that sense homosexuality is not separate from various sexual sins but is a form of those sins. Separate or not, the scriptures are clear that it is

---

[4] The Hebrew word translated in Deuteronomy 23:17 as sodomite in the King James Bible is qadesh, a male devotee to licentious idolatry. It specifically refers to male temple prostitutes.

contrary to God's created design for sexual expression and is, therefore, sin.

It is important that you understand that having same-sex attraction is not a sin. It isn't even temptation. You did not choose to have that attraction. That is not to say, however, that because you did not choose it that you were born with it or that God made you that way. There is no question that same-sex attraction is contrary to God's created design for male and female. The sin is in acting on that same-sex attraction as discussed above. You need to repent of the homosexual sin and seek healing for the same-sex attraction. We'll discuss this in greater detail in another chapter. In the next chapter, we will look at the scriptures in which homosexual sin is at least believed to be mentioned.

CHAPTER 5 - WHAT THE SCRIPTURES SAY ABOUT HOMOSEXUALITY

In many Christian circles there is considerable debate over what God's word says about homosexuality. Since the remaining chapters of this book are applications of God's word, we need to examine what the Bible says about homosexuality. Particularly since much of the Church's response to homosexuality - and to homosexuals themselves - is presumably based on the scriptures. As those who struggle with same-sex attraction, it is especially important for us to have a proper understanding of what God's word says about both our attraction and our acting on that attraction. Now, I'm not going to get into a detailed discussion of what has been called gay or pro-gay theology or to use this chapter to simply explain why that theology is wrong; and I'm not particularly interested in addressing the gay political agenda. There are other books on the market that do that quite well and there really isn't much new that I can add to that; even though it is erroneous to say that there is one set of beliefs, one theology, in which all pro-homosexual faiths believe or one set of political beliefs held by every homosexual. I will, however, in the course of explaining what I believe the scriptures say about homosexual behavior, use examples of teaching that I heard and taught when I was a minister in the National Gay Pentecostal Alliance, as a contrast to the truth of God's word. So, let's get to it.

THE NECESSITY OF TAKING SCRIPTURES IN CONTEXT

Many Christians tend to be a bit lazy when it comes to our use of God's word. We quote a particular scripture to prove our point but ignore the context of the passage in which it is contained. For example, we're quick to tell unbelievers that God stands at the door of their hearts knocking but ignore the fact that the Lord wasn't saying that to unbelievers at all. Rather, He was saying it to a fallen, backslidden Church (see Revelation 3:14-22). We also tend to use scripture with improper motives. One of the most common criticisms that pro-homosexual faiths have of us is our selective use of scripture to prove a point; and I believe that particular criticism is valid even though the same charge can rightly be made against pro-homosexual faiths (or worse: many of them deny the authority and inerrancy of scripture). We particularly tend to be rather selective when it comes to quoting from the Law of Moses. We are quick to tell homosexuals that the scriptures call for their deaths (see Leviticus 20:13), but are unwilling to say it to children who rebel against their parents (see Deuteronomy 21:19-23). It is absolutely essential, if we are to be, "rightly dividing the word of truth" (2 Timothy 2:15), that we pay attention to the context of the scriptures we are quoting. Now, there's nothing wrong with quoting a single verse or part of a verse but we need to do so in a way that is true to the context of the passage in which it is contained. Failure to do so is nothing less than the sin of bearing false witness - in this case, against the word of God itself.

THE LAW OF MOSES AND THE CHRISTIAN

The strongest prohibitions against homosexual behavior are contained in those sections of scripture we refer to collectively as the Law of Moses (referred to as such because they are part of the law that God gave Moses to lay down for the fledgling nation of Israel). That law is what is contained in the Old Testament books of Leviticus and Deuteronomy (Exodus and Numbers are mainly a historical record). Jesus seems, however to have made a distinction between the Ten Commandments, found in Exodus 20, and the Law of Moses in Leviticus and Deuteronomy. He summarized the ten into two (see Matthew 22:37 and its companions in Mark and Luke). He said that He did not come to abolish the Law of Moses, but to fulfill it (Matthew 5:17; fulfill, as used here, means to make replete or to bring to completion - all that the Law was meant to accomplish was accomplished in Jesus). But what place does the Law of Moses have in the lives of Christians? Are we bound by the law or is it entirely irrelevant? The way many Christians apply the law to homosexuals, one would think that we are bound by the law. Other Christians claim that we are to ignore the law as being entirely irrelevant and won't so much as open their Bibles to any part of the Old Testament. Who's right? Who's wrong? Both.

We need to remember that the only Bible the Christians in the first century had was what we call the

Old Testament. It wasn't until the Apostles recorded onto parchment what the Lord taught them that we began to have other scriptures. It is clear that what they wrote was intended to have the authority of scripture. Brother Peter wrote in his second epistle about Brother Paul's writings, "As also in all his epistles, speaking in them of these things; in which are some things hard to be understood, which they that are unlearned and unstable wrest, as they do also the other scriptures, unto their own destruction" (2 Peter 3:16). The Old Testament, in the first century Church, was what they relied on as the written revelation of God. For them, all of it was relevant in their day: not only for Jewish Christians but for Gentile Christians as well. As Brother Paul wrote to a Gentile Christian pastor in 2 Timothy 3:16-17, "All scripture is given by inspiration of God, and is profitable for doctrine, for reproof, for correction, for instruction in righteousness: that the man of God may be perfect, thoroughly furnished unto all good works." So, we can't just scrap the Old Testament as being irrelevant to our walk with the Lord. But, does every scripture apply to every believer in every [5]dispensation?

---

[5] Use of the word "dispensation" here presumes a belief in the doctrine of dispensationalism. That doctrine is thoroughly explained in Brother C. I. Scofield's book Rightly Dividing The Word Of Truth and in Brother Clarence Larkin's book Dispensational Truth.

THE FIRST CHURCH COUNCIL

Too many Christians ignore the New Testament book of Acts, even though it contains the major history of the first century Church and shows how the Apostles put into practice what Jesus taught; especially concerning the doctrine of salvation. They'll quote from the third chapter of Brother John's gospel or the tenth chapter of Brother Paul's letter to the Romans while ignoring the second, eighth and tenth chapters of Acts. For those of us who do not ignore Acts, there was a controversy in the Church over the very issue we are discussing here: the place of the Law of Moses in the lives of Gentile Christians. Here is the text of what occurred at what I call the first Church council. The text is Acts 15:1-29.

"And certain men which came down from Judaea taught the brethren, and said, 'Except ye be circumcised after the manner of Moses, ye cannot be saved.' When therefore Paul and Barnabas had no small dissension and disputation with them, they determined that Paul and Barnabas, and certain other of them, should go up to Jerusalem unto the apostles and elders about this question. And being brought on their way by the church, they passed through Phenice and Samaria, declaring the conversion of the Gentiles: and they caused great joy unto all the brethren. And when they were come to Jerusalem, they were received of the church, and of the apostles and elders, and they declared

all things that God had done with them. But
there rose up certain of the sect of the Pharisees
which believed, saying that it was needful to
circumcise them, and to command them to keep
the law of Moses. And the apostles and elders
came together for to consider of this matter.
And when there had been much disputing, Peter
rose up, and said unto them, 'Men and brethren,
ye know how that a good while ago God made
choice among us, that the Gentiles by my mouth
should hear the word of the gospel, and believe.
And God, which knoweth the hearts, bare them
witness, giving them the Holy Ghost, even as he
did unto us; and put no difference between us
and them, purifying their hearts by faith. Now
therefore why tempt ye God, to put a yoke upon
the neck of the disciples, which neither our
fathers nor we were able to bear? But we
believe that through the grace of the Lord Jesus
Christ we shall be saved, even as they.' Then
all the multitude kept silence, and gave audience
to Barnabas and Paul, declaring what miracles
and wonders God had wrought among the
Gentiles by them. And after they had held their
peace, James answered, saying, 'Men and
brethren, hearken unto me: Simeon hath
declared how God at the first did visit the
Gentiles, to take out of them a people for his
name. And to this agree the words of the
prophets; as it is written, "After this I will
return, and will build again the tabernacle of
David, which is fallen down; and I will build

again the ruins thereof, and I will set it up: that the residue of men might seek after the Lord, and all the Gentiles, upon whom my name is called, saith the Lord, who doeth all these things. Known unto God are all his works from the beginning of the world." Wherefore my sentence is, that we trouble not them, which from among the Gentiles are turned to God: but that we write unto them, that they abstain from pollutions of idols, and from fornication, and from things strangled, and from blood. For Moses of old time hath in every city them that preach him, being read in the synagogues every sabbath day.' Then pleased it the apostles and elders, with the whole church, to send chosen men of their own company to Antioch with Paul and Barnabas; namely, Judas surnamed Barsabas, and Silas, chief men among the brethren: and they wrote letters by them after this manner; 'The apostles and elders and brethren send greeting unto the brethren which are of the Gentiles in Antioch and Syria and Cilicia: forasmuch as we have heard, that certain which went out from us have troubled you with words, subverting your souls, saying, Ye must be circumcised, and keep the law: to whom we gave no such commandment: it seemed good unto us, being assembled with one accord, to send chosen men unto you with our beloved Barnabas and Paul, men that have hazarded their lives for the name of our Lord Jesus Christ. We have sent therefore Judas and Silas, who shall also tell you the same things by mouth. For it seemed good to the Holy Ghost, and to us, to lay upon you no greater burden than these necessary things; that ye abstain from meats offered to idols, and from blood, and from things strangled, and from fornication: from which if ye keep yourselves, ye shall do well. Fare ye well."

There is a popular doctrine in the Church today that teaches that the above text is about keeping the ceremonial law and, specifically, circumcision; and that this was not about the moral law. Let me state clearly that the context of the passage does not support such a doctrine. Notice what Brother Peter said in Acts 15:10, "Now therefore why tempt ye God, to put a yoke upon the neck of the disciples, which neither our fathers nor we were able to bear?" Keeping the "ceremonial law" - the various ordinances about circumcision, food, sacrifices, clothing, etc. - was the part of the law that they were able to keep. It was the "moral law," - the various ordinances about behavior - that they were unable to keep. If they were able to keep the moral law, there would have been no need for Jesus to even come to Earth and die on the cross: the Law of Moses would have been enough to bring salvation. Now, I don't happen to believe that the Lord Himself makes such a distinction between ceremonial and moral law that we make. Rather, I think that all of it was moral in the sense that it was all part of God's specific covenant with the nation of Israel as it was called to be a people holy unto the

Lord. Acts 15 makes it abundantly clear that the Law of Moses does not apply to Gentiles.

So, what does apply to Gentiles? The answer comes from the [6]bishop of the Jerusalem church, Brother [7]James in Acts 15:19-21, "Wherefore my sentence is, that we trouble not them, which from among the Gentiles are turned to God: but that we write unto them, that they abstain from pollutions of idols, and from fornication, and from things strangled, and from blood. For Moses of old time hath in every city them that preach him, being read in the synagogues every sabbath day." Brother Paul, who brought his arguments against requiring the Gentiles to keep the Law of Moses to the Jerusalem council, dealt with this issue of the law extensively in his epistle to the Romans. I urge you to study it for yourself.

We need to be careful how we apply scriptures to particular groups or situations. The passages in Leviticus and Deuteronomy prohibiting homosexual

---

[6] Bishop, as I use it here, refers to the word as it is used in 1 Timothy 3:1-2 (KJV) and not as it is used in the Roman Catholic Church.

[7] The name of those men in the New Testament rendered in English Bibles as James is really the Hebrew name Ya'aqob and is rendered in the Old Testament as Jacob. In the Greek New Testament, the name is rendered Iakobos. James is an English name that is similar in meaning to Ya'aqob and Iakobos: one who supplants. It was unnecessary to use the English name James when the English translation of Ya'aqob and Iakobos - Jacob - would have been more accurate. It may have been more than coincidental that the translators appointed by King James used his name in the New Testament instead of the English form of Iakobos.

behavior are part of the Law of Moses and, therefore, are for the Jews. Homosexual behavior is, however, included in the prohibitions that the Jerusalem council established for Gentile believers, in the Council's use of the word "fornication." All sex outside of God's created order of marriage between a man and a woman would fall under the sin of fornication, and that includes sexual activity between people of the same gender. Yes, "All scripture is given by inspiration of God, and is profitable for doctrine, for reproof, for correction, for instruction in righteousness; that the man of God may be perfect, thoroughly furnished unto all good works" (2 Timothy 3:16). No, there is not any part of God's word that is irrelevant. But the word of God can only serve its purpose if we use it properly. We can't just go around randomly applying scriptures to every situation. To do so is to bear false witness against what the word of God says. As we will see, there are scriptures that apply to homosexual behavior; but we need to be careful in knowing what to apply and when. In the rest of this chapter we'll look at those scriptures.

THE SIN OF SODOM

Christian tradition teaches that Sodom, Gomorrah and the cities of the plain were destroyed specifically because of homosexuality (see Matthew 15:6 regarding men's traditions). That teaching is based on an event that was highlighted in the passage that tells about the destruction of those cities. In that event, the men of Sodom gathered outside Lot's door demanding that he send out his two male guests (who the men of Sodom did not know were angels from heaven) so that they could sexually abuse them. Since there are many Christians who are today using this story as an example of how God would someday judge America for supporting homosexuality and allowing it to be presented to our school children as a valid lifestyle choice, I think we need to take a closer look at what the Biblical account really says. The entire story is found in Genesis 18:16-19:29, though most of us seem to ignore the parts of the story contained in Genesis 18. Here is the text of the story.

"And the men rose up from thence, and looked toward Sodom: and Abraham went with them to bring them on the way. And the [8]LORD said, Shall I hide from Abraham that thing which I do; Seeing that Abraham shall surely become a great and mighty nation, and all the nations of the earth shall be blessed in him? For I know him, that he will command his children and his household after him, and they shall keep the way of the LORD, to do justice and judgment; that the LORD may bring upon Abraham that which he hath spoken of him. And the LORD said, Because the cry of Sodom and Gomorrah is great, and because their sin is very grievous; I will go down now, and see

---

[8] God's Hebrew name, of which the closest English approximation is YHVH, is used wherever the King James (and some other English translations) uses LORD in all capital letters.

whether they have done altogether according to the cry of it, which is come unto me; and if not, I will know. And the men turned their faces from thence, and went toward Sodom: but Abraham stood yet before the LORD. And Abraham drew near, and said, Wilt thou also destroy the righteous with the wicked? Peradventure there be fifty righteous within the city: wilt thou also destroy and not spare the place for the fifty righteous that *are* therein? That be far from thee to do after this manner, to slay the righteous with the wicked: and that the righteous should be as the wicked, that be far from thee: Shall not the Judge of all the earth do right? And the LORD said, If I find in Sodom fifty righteous within the city, then I will spare all the place for their sakes. And Abraham answered and said, Behold now, I have taken upon me to speak unto the Lord, which *am but* dust and ashes: Peradventure there shall lack five of the fifty righteous: wilt thou destroy all the city for *lack of* five? And he said, If I find there forty and five, I will not destroy *it*. And he spake unto him yet again, and said, Peradventure there shall be forty found there. And he said, I will not do *it* for forty's sake. And he said *unto him*, Oh let not the Lord be angry, and I will speak: Peradventure there shall thirty be found there. And he said, I will not do *it*, if I find thirty there. And he said, Behold now, I have taken upon me to speak unto the Lord: Peradventure there shall be twenty found there. And he said, I will not destroy *it* for twenty's sake. And he said, Oh let not the Lord be angry, and I will speak yet but this once: Peradventure ten shall be found there. And he said, I will not destroy *it* for ten's sake. And the LORD went his way, as soon as he had left communing with Abraham: and Abraham returned unto his place. And there came two angels to Sodom at even; and Lot sat in the gate of Sodom: and Lot seeing *them* rose up to meet them; and he bowed himself with his face toward the ground; And he said, Behold now, my lords, turn in, I pray you, into your servant's house, and tarry all night, and wash your feet, and ye shall rise up early, and go on your ways. And they said, Nay; but we will abide in the street all night. And he pressed upon them greatly; and they turned in unto him, and entered into his house; and he made them a feast, and did bake unleavened bread, and they did eat. But before they lay down, the men of the city, *even* the men of Sodom, compassed the house round, both old and young, all the people from every quarter: And they called unto Lot, and said unto him, Where *are* the men which came in to thee this night? bring them out unto us, that we may know them. And Lot went out at the door unto them, and shut the door after him, And said, I pray you, brethren, do not so wickedly. Behold now, I have two daughters which have not known man; let me, I pray you, bring them out unto you, and do ye to them as *is* good in your eyes: only unto these men do nothing; for therefore came they under the shadow of my roof. And they said, Stand back. And they said *again*, This one *fellow* came in to sojourn, and he will needs be a judge: now will we deal worse with thee, than with them. And they pressed sore upon the man, *even* Lot, and came near to break the door. But the men put forth their hand, and pulled Lot into the house to them, and shut to the door. And they smote the men that *were* at the door of the house with blindness, both small and great: so that they wearied themselves to find the door. And the men said unto Lot, Hast thou here any besides? son in law, and thy sons, and thy daughters, and whatsoever thou hast in the city, bring *them* out of this place: For we will destroy this place, because the cry of them is waxen great before the face of the LORD; and the LORD hath sent us to destroy it. And Lot went out, and spake unto his sons in law, which married his daughters, and said, Up, get you out of this place; for the LORD will destroy this city. But he seemed as one that mocked unto his sons in law. And when the morning arose, then the angels hastened Lot, saying, Arise, take thy wife, and thy two daughters, which are here; lest thou be consumed in the iniquity of the city. And while he lingered, the men laid hold upon his hand, and upon the hand of his wife, and upon the hand of his two daughters; the LORD being merciful unto him: and they brought him forth, and set him without the city. And it came to pass, when they had brought them forth abroad, that he said, Escape for thy life; look not behind thee, neither stay thou in all the plain; escape to the mountain, lest thou be consumed. And Lot said unto them, Oh, not so, my Lord: Behold now, thy servant hath found grace in thy sight, and thou hast magnified thy mercy, which thou hast shewed unto me in saving my life; and I cannot escape to the mountain, lest some evil take me, and I die: Behold now, this city *is* near to flee unto, and it *is* a little one: Oh, let me escape thither, (*is* it not a little one?) and my soul shall live. And he said unto him, See, I have accepted thee concerning this thing also, that I will not overthrow this city, for the which thou hast spoken. Haste thee, escape thither; for I cannot do any thing till thou be come thither. Therefore the name of the city was called Zoar. The sun was risen upon the earth when Lot entered into Zoar. Then the LORD rained upon Sodom and upon Gomorrah brimstone and fire from the LORD out of heaven; And he overthrew those cities, and all the plain, and all the inhabitants of the cities, and that which grew upon the ground. But his wife looked back from behind him, and she became a pillar of salt. And Abraham gat up early in the morning to the place where he stood before the LORD: And he looked toward Sodom and Gomorrah, and toward all the land of the plain, and beheld, and, lo, the smoke of the country went up as the smoke of a furnace. And it came to pass, when God destroyed the cities of the plain, that God remembered Abraham, and sent Lot out of the midst of the overthrow, when he overthrew the cities in the which Lot dwelt."

No matter how many times I read the text, I simply am unable to see how Sodom, Gomorrah and the cities of the plain were destroyed specifically because of homosexual behavior that did not actually occur. It is clear that the Lord had already determined before the attempted gang rape to destroy those places. The only thing that would have kept God from destroying the cities of the plain was the presence of 10 or more righteous people. I believe it wouldn't have made any difference if the two angels hadn't gone to Sodom: the cities would still have been destroyed. The only people for whom the presence of the angels made a difference were Lot, his two young daughters, and the people of Zoar for whom Lot pleaded as he asked the angels to let him escape to that city. (Notice, however, that Lot didn't stay there long: he became afraid and decided to flee to the mountains where the angels had originally told him to flee. Lesson: when an angel of the Lord tells you to go somewhere, go directly there. Do not pass Go. Do not collect 200 dollars.) Let's look for a moment at the attempted gang rape that so many of us point to as the homosexuality for which the cities of the plain were supposedly destroyed.

"But before they lay down, the men of the city, even the men of Sodom, compassed the house round, both old and young, all the people from every quarter: And they called unto Lot, and said unto him, Where are the men which came in to thee this night? bring them out unto us, that we may know them" (Genesis 19:4-5).

Notice what is says here: "both old and young, all the people from every quarter" (Genesis 19:4). It seems that it wasn't just the males in Sodom who went to Lot's house that night but "all the people from every quarter." But, how can we be sure? Why does it matter? If it were only the males of the city, it gives more credence to the view that their intent was to gang rape Lot's visitors: having the women and children suggests otherwise to gay and pro-gay theologians but their presence clearly didn't make a difference. Let's take this passage again, this time inserting the Hebrew word in place of men and people.

"But before they lay down, the *enowsh* of the city, even the *enowsh* of Sodom, compassed the house round, both old and young, all the *am* from every quarter: And they called unto Lot, and said unto him, Where are the *enowsh* which came in to thee this night? bring them out unto us, that we may know them" (Genesis 19:4-5).

Enowsh is a Hebrew word that properly means a mortal; hence, a man in general (singly or collectively). It comes from *anash*, a primitive root; to be frail, feeble, or, figuratively, melancholy, and indicates man in his mortality. According to Strong's

Exhaustive Concordance, the meaning of *enowsh* is often unexpressed in the English versions, especially when used in [9]apposition with another word. That the men of Sodom themselves used *enowsh* makes it clear that they thought the two angels were just as human as they. Notice also that it wasn't all the *enowsh* that surrounded Lot's house but, rather, all the *am*. The Hebrew word *am* is one that means a people as a congregated unit; specifically, a tribe (as those of Israel); hence, collectively, troops or attendants; figuratively, a flock. I believe that when the people of Sodom found out that these two men came into town and went into Lot's house, they thought that Lot and the two men were plotting some dastardly deed against them - that these men were spies and/or terrorists (whatever the equivalent of these was at the time). When you're as evil as the people of Sodom clearly were, you tend to expect visitors to your city to have ulterior motives and, so, you don't trust them. Here was Lot: a foreigner bringing two other foreigners into his home. In the minds of the people of Sodom, of course these men were up to no good - and they weren't about to let them cause any trouble. So, they all surrounded Lot's house and demanded that he bring the two foreigners he was harboring out to them. Let's go back to the text.

---

[9] Apposition is the placing of a word or expression beside another so that the second explains and has the same grammatical construction as the first; or is the relationship between such terms, e.g., my friend, Joe.

"But before they lay down, the men of the city, even the men of Sodom, compassed the house round, both old and young, all the people from every quarter: And they called unto Lot, and said unto him, 'Where are the men which came in to thee this night? bring them out unto us, that we may know them.' And Lot went out at the door unto them, and shut the door after him, And said, 'I pray you, brethren, do not so wickedly. Behold now, I have two daughters which have not known man; let me, I pray you, bring them out unto you, and do ye to them as is good in your eyes: only unto these men do nothing; for therefore came they under the shadow of my roof.' And they said, 'Stand back.' And they said again, 'This one fellow came in to sojourn, and he will needs be a judge: now will we deal worse with thee, than with them.' And they pressed sore upon the man, even Lot, and came near to break the door" (Genesis 19:4-9).

Even without looking at the original Hebrew, it's clear what the men who spoke to Lot wanted to do to his guests just from Lot's response to their demand. They wanted to gang rape and brutalize Lot's guests and he offered them his two virgin daughters in their place - a perfectly appropriate response in a time when females were not much more than property. Lot's male guests were to be protected even at the expense of the females in his household. It is on this event that the various interpretations of the story hinge.

Specifically, the controversy is about the meaning of one Hebrew verb, translated in the King James as "to know." Pro-gay theology, including my former denomination, argues that "to know" isn't used here in a sexual context. The verb is *yada* and it does have a variety of uses in the Old Testament - including as a euphemism for having sex. According to Strong's Exhaustive Concordance, *yada* is a primitive root; to know (properly, to ascertain by seeing); used in a great variety of senses, figuratively, literally, euphemistically and inferentially (including observation, care, recognition; and causatively, instruction, designation, punishment, etc.). To find out how it is being used in a particular instance, you have to pay attention to the grammatical context. (This is where you apply those English comprehension skills you learned in elementary and secondary school). You don't tell people who just want to know the identity and business of the foreigners you're harboring, "I pray you, brethren, do not so wickedly" (Genesis 19:7). Again, it's clear that *yada* was used as a euphemism for having sex in this instance because Lot offered his virgin daughters ("which have not known [10]man") in the place of his male guests. To say that the men of Sodom wanted anything other than to gang rape - to forcibly have sex with - Lot's male guests is to bear false witness against the word of God. But that

---

[10] Man, used here, is the Hebrew word iysh and means a man as an individual or a male person (the same word used to describe what Adam was to Eve). That this particular word is used for man herein conjunction with yada, makes it clear that Lot was saying his daughters were virgins.

attempted gang rape is not why those cities were destroyed. So, why were Sodom, Gomorrah and the cities of the plain destroyed? What was the sin of Sodom?

There is absolutely no question that the cities of the plain were evil beyond comparison. Genesis 13:13 tells us, "But the men of Sodom were wicked and sinners before the LORD exceedingly." Notice what the Lord told Abraham in Genesis 18:20-21 well before the attempted gang rape, "And the LORD said, 'Because the cry of Sodom and Gomorrah is great, and because their sin is very grievous; I will go down now, and see whether they have done altogether according to the cry of it, which is come unto me; and if not, I will know." Sodom and Gomorrah were so evil that the Lord felt it necessary to go down and see it for Himself before destroying them. Christian tradition (which makes "the word of God of none effect") focuses on the attempted gang rape of Lot's guests and says that homosexuality was why the cities of the plain were destroyed. Pro-gay theology says that the sin of Sodom was extreme inhospitality - supposedly a very serious offense in those ancient Middle Eastern cultures. I think they're both wrong. Please consider the following:

- The attempted gang rape took place in Sodom. If this act was the reason for God destroying all of the cities of the plain, doesn't this make God unjust in that He decimated entire populations for one act merely attempted by the population of one city?

- God had already acknowledged that the cities of the plain were so evil as to warrant their destruction but Christian tradition would make us think that they were so evil because of only one sin that actually never took place. God sent the two angels to Sodom to confirm what He already knew to be true. If the attempted gang rape that is interpreted to be homosexuality was the reason for their destruction, aren't the angels guilty of entrapment inasmuch as the attempted gang rape would never have taken place had they not gone to Sodom?

I believe that scripture interprets scripture. With that in mind, let's go to the one place where the reasons for the destruction of the cities of the plain are specifically identified: Ezekiel 16:48-50.

"As I live, saith the Lord [11]GOD, Sodom thy sister hath not done, she nor her daughters, as thou hast done, thou and thy daughters. Behold, this was the iniquity of thy sister Sodom, pride, fullness of bread, and abundance of idleness was in her and in her daughters, neither did she strengthen the hand of the poor and needy. And they were haughty, and committed abomination before me: therefore I took them away as I saw good."

---

[11] A form of God's Hebrew name is used here.

Pro-gay theology usually leaves out verse 50 and says that the passage proves that God destroyed the cities of the plain because of inhospitality - thereby bearing false witness against the word of God. But let's look at verse 50, since it is part of the list of reasons the Lord Himself cites for the destruction of those cities: "And they were haughty, and committed abomination before me: therefore I took them away as I saw good." Christian tradition says that verse 50 proves that God destroyed the cities of the plain because of homosexuality by claiming that the abomination the people in the cities committed was homosexuality (and by claiming that homosexuality is the only sin identified in scripture as an abomination). It is exactly because of this kind of disagreement that we absolutely must pay attention to the grammatical context. We need to stop being so lazy when it comes to simple English comprehension; pro-gay theology and Christian tradition are equally guilty of this. Such laziness is clearly in violation of those scriptures that tell us to rightly divide the word of truth and to study to show ourselves approved unto God, and bears false witness against His word. No, there is no evidence that the cities of the plain were destroyed because they violated unwritten cultural laws regarding hospitality or because the people supposedly lived a homosexual lifestyle. They were destroyed because they were so evil that the only solution was to completely eradicate them - just like the condition of humanity right before the flood. The list in Ezekiel 16:48-50 seems rather benign and not unlike Euro-American culture today, until you consider the meaning of the word abomination as it is used in the Old Testament.

The Hebrew word translated as abomination is *towebah*. Properly, it means something disgusting morally, i.e., as a noun, an abhorrence; especially idolatry or, concretely, an idol. As abomination, it is used 112 times in the Old Testament, mostly in connection with idolatry and idolatrous practices. Among the idolatrous practices in that part of the world at the time was what was later referred to as passing one's children through the fire. Molech was an idol with outstretched arms under which a fire was kindled. Babies were placed in the arms of Molech and sacrificed. In addition, the people in the cities of the plain may have practiced cannibalism and/or bestiality, depending on the correct translation of two Greek words in Jude 7, *heteros sarx* (other flesh/meat). These would certainly qualify as morally disgusting, as abomination. Whatever the specific abomination was, there is no question from the context that it was something directly associated with idolatrous practices; but there is no evidence that it was specifically homosexuality.

To this conclusion some might be inclined to respond, "Brother, you're still holding onto the beliefs of your former gay denomination because you say the cities of the plain were not destroyed for their homosexuality. You haven't left the homosexual lifestyle at all." To which I challenge you to take off the blinders of tradition and examine the scriptures for yourselves (and note that I also disagreed here with what pro-gay theology, including my former denomination, taught about this). If I'm wrong in saying that the cities of the plain were not destroyed because of homosexuality, then show me how I'm wrong. Again, it all goes back to taking scriptures in context instead of committing the sin of proof texting. Let's look at the remaining scriptures that mention (or are said to mention) homosexual behavior. This time, rather than reprinting the texts here, I ask you to go get your Bible and open it to the respective passages as we discuss them.

LEVITICUS 18:22 and 20:13 - These are two of the most commonly used texts against homosexuality. We've already discussed earlier the place the Law of Moses has in the lives of Gentile Christians and these two passages are part of the Law of Moses. There is, however, another bone of contention about the use of these two passages: the English translation. The King James and some other English translations contain the phrase "as with womankind," meaning that men weren't allowed to have sex with men the way they were supposed to with women in the context of marriage. I tend to be a literalist when it comes to translating from one language to another and the Hebrew equivalent of "as with" is not in the text. The word mistranslated "as with" is *mishkab*, a bed (figuratively, a bier); abstractly, sleep; by euphemism, carnal intercourse. The National Gay Pentecostal Alliance taught that this only prohibits where men can have sex with men, that a woman's bed was her own and that even her husband couldn't go there except during certain times. Again, the literalist in me would rather see the English Bibles translate the Hebrew and Greek more literally than they do. But, let's look at this more closely. The passages tell us that a man may not lie with - the Hebrew word is *sh'kobeth*, a [sexual] lying with - another man. Does the rest of the passage mean that he is prohibited from lying with other men entirely or only prohibited from doing so in a woman's bed? Let's look back at the word mistranslated "as with." *Mishkab* comes from *shakab*, a primitive root: to lie down (for rest, sexual connection, decease or any other purpose). The context of the passage makes it clear that *mishkab* is being used as a euphemism for carnal intercourse. Further evidence of this comes from a tidy little detail that the National Gay Pentecostal Alliance leaves out: that the root of *sh'kobeth* is *shakab*, the same as of *mishkab*. There is no evidence in scripture that says a woman's bed was her own and that even her husband could only go there during certain times, other than the prohibition during a woman's menstrual cycle - particularly when you consider that women in ancient times were little more than property. While "as with" is a mistranslation of *mishkab*, it renders the passage correctly in the sense of showing - as the Hebrew does - that men were prohibited from lying carnally with other men.

DEUTERONOMY 23:17 - This passage is an example of the unfortunate insertion of tradition into translation. The English word sodomite has come to be associated with homosexuality (and with any sexual intercourse held to be abnormal) but is an inaccurate association because, as I have already shown, Sodom was not destroyed because of homosexuality. The real definition of sodomite is simply a person from the city of Sodom. The Hebrew word used in this passage for sodomite is *qadesh*, a (quasi) sacred person, i.e. (technically) a (male) devotee (by prostitution) to licentious idolatry. (The Hebrew word translated as whore is the feminine form of *qadesh*). This passage, rather than being a prohibition of homosexual behavior in general, is a prohibition of temple prostitution - male and female devotees to certain idols who sold sexual favors to worshippers as part of pagan fertility rites that were commonly practiced among the Canaanites and other peoples of the region. Whether these sexual favors were sold to others of their own gender or not, I'm not certain, though Romans 1:26-27 suggests that this was same-sex prostitution since Brother Paul was writing about the same kind of idolatrous practice that occurred especially in the temples in Corinth from which he wrote Romans. Regardless of whether this was same-sex prostitution or opposite-sex prostitution, Deuteronomy 23:18 makes it clear that the practice was morally disgusting, an abomination, and was prohibited accordingly.

JUDGES 19:22-29 - This event is similar to the attempted gang rape that so many Christians call homosexuality and believe was the reason Sodom and the other cities of the plain were destroyed. In this passage, however, the men took the Levite's concubine, "and they knew her, and abused her all the night until the morning" (Judges 19:25). In an act too brutal to describe in detail, the men actually took the

Levite's concubine in the place of the Levite himself (the one they really wanted to rape). They did what the men of Sodom were kept from doing and, yet, it was Sodom that God destroyed and not Gibeah. There is absolutely no question that the intent of these men was to rape and violently abuse the Levite sexually: they took his concubine instead. As with the Sodom story, pro-gay theology argues that the men of Gibeah were simply violating some unwritten code regarding hospitality. Most Christians argue that this passage is about homosexuality since the men of Gibeah wanted to have sex with the old man's male Levite guest. Again, being the literalist that I am, there is no other way of interpreting this passage than to say that a bunch of guys were out partying and getting drunk and they went to this old man's house demanding that he send out his Levite guest so that they could rape him. This doesn't say anything about the sexual orientation of these men. In fact, thousands of male prisoners around the world - heterosexual and non-heterosexual - engage in exactly the same raping of other men today. The passage is one about horrendously violent rape and sexual abuse, not sexual orientation or even specifically homosexual behavior. It's amazing how we focus on what the men of Gibeah intended instead of on what they did. We get so hung up on the fact that these drunken men wanted to rape the old man's male Levite guest instead of the fact that they did rape his concubine. It was the result of the rape and fatal brutalization of the Levite's concubine (she died as a result of her injuries) that the entire tribe of Benjamin was almost exterminated by the other tribes, not the fact that the men of Gibeah wanted to have sex with the Levite himself.

RUTH AND NAOMI - There is no question that the story of Ruth and her mother-in-law Naomi is a beautiful example of filial loyalty. Many gay theologians, however, want us to see this as a lesbian relationship. In doing so, they ignore the fact that Naomi was the mother of Ruth's husband. There is no question that Ruth was devoted to her mother-in-law, but there was nothing romantic or sexual about that devotion. It is unfortunate that the beautiful words in Ruth 1:16-17 are used in weddings today because such use gives gay theologians justification in applying them to a lesbian relationship. Here are those words from the King James Bible. "And Ruth said, Intreat me not to leave thee, or to return from following after thee: for whither thou goest, I will go; and where thou lodgest, I will lodge: thy people shall be my people, and thy God my God: Where thou diest, will I die, and there will I be buried: the LORD do so to me, and more also, if ought but death part thee and me." Ruth was prepared to leave behind everything - including her familial, national and cultural identity - to stay with her mother-in-law. She was prepared to fully adopt the nation, culture and faith of her mother-in-law because of the filial devotion that Ruth had for her. No, this is not a lesbian relationship.

DAVID AND JONATHAN - This is another relationship that gay theologians insist was homosexual in nature. The primary passage of scripture that is at issue here is 1 Samuel 18. The first four verses tell us about the relationship between these two men: that "the soul of Jonathan was knit with the soul of David, and Jonathan loved him as his own soul" (1 Samuel 18:1). Let's look at this more closely. The Hebrew word translated here as soul is *nephesh*: properly, a breathing creature, i.e. animal of (abstractly) vitality; used very widely in a literal, accommodated or figurative sense (bodily or mental). It's the same word used in Genesis 2:7 to denote what the first human had become when God breathed into him the breath of life. The soul, contrary to popular belief, is the combination of body and spirit - humans don't have souls: they are living souls. The National Gay Pentecostal Alliance taught that it is the use of *nephesh* that proves Jonathan's love for David had a sexual element to it. Such a view would seemingly be given credence by the Hebrew word translated in 1 Samuel 18:1 as loved, *ahab* or *raheb*; a primitive root: to have affection for (sexually or otherwise). But it only seemingly lends credence to that argument because the word is also translated like and friend, the context determining how it is used just as with *yada*. We also must look at what Jonathan and David did. In 1 Samuel 18:4 they made a covenant with each other. To seal that covenant, Jonathan took off all those things that showed him to be a military man, and a man of authority, and gave them to David. He was, in effect, surrendering his position to David. This is clear from 1 Samuel 18:5 in that Saul put David in authority over the military. Much is also made of 1 Samuel 18:21, where David was to become Saul's son-in-law "in *the one of* the twain," and the fact that the phrase *the one of* is [12]italicized in the King James, meaning that it doesn't appear in the original Hebrew. The argument made by the National Gay Pentecostal Alliance is that David entered into marriage covenants with two children of Saul. In 1 Samuel 18:27 we see that David did marry Saul's daughter Michal. The argument is made that David never married Merab and that this raises the question of what other child of Saul would have married David, to which they answer that the other marriage was to Jonathan. However, since engagement or betrothal had the same legal effect as marriage, and Saul had betrothed Merab to David, Merab was legally David's fiancée and, therefore, David was Saul's son-in-law because of her. There is no evidence that the covenant between Jonathan and David was a marriage covenant. In fact, David's objections to being the king's son-in-law would be a clear indication that his covenant with Jonathan was not a marriage covenant. There is more to the story of Jonathan and David from which my former denomination argues, along with various gay theologians, that their relationship was at least a sexual relationship if not a marriage; but I won't go into those here. Suffice it to say that David and Jonathan were not weeping together and holding and kissing each other in 1 Samuel 20:41 until David achieved an

---

[12] Words in the King James Bible and New American Standard Bible that are in italics are not found in the original Hebrew, Aramaic or Greek. They are added to make the English translation grammatically correct, though sometimes the addition of these words changes the meaning of the passage.

erection (the supposed translation of the Hebrew word translated in the King James as exceeded; it is literally translated "to become large"). Suffice it also to say that David's reference to Jonathan as his brother in 2 Samuel 1:26 is clear evidence that the relationship was of friendship, not marriage - a friendship that David valued more than his sexual/romantic love for women (a comparison that my former denomination insists was further proof that what Jonathan and David had was a sexual relationship).

DANIEL AND ASHPHENAZ - As far as I know, only the National Gay Pentecostal Alliance taught that these two men were married homosexual lovers. At issue is a single verse of scripture, Daniel 1:9, "Now God had brought Daniel into favour and tender love with the prince of the eunuchs." The argument is that God played matchmaker and put these two into a same-sex marriage, and that this is evidenced by the Hebrew words for favour and tender love. The Hebrew word for favour is *checed*, meaning kindness; by implication (toward God) piety: rarely (by opposition) reproof, or (subjectively) beauty. The word for the phrase tender love is *racham*, meaning compassion (in the plural, *rachamim*); by extension, the womb (as cherishing the fetus); by implication, a maiden. The National Gay Pentecostal Alliance argues that this latter word is redundant if it means something similar to *checed*, so it has to mean something else and one of those possible meanings is love. They further argue that the root letters of *racham* are r-ch-m and that all Hebrew words with those root letters would have similar meaning. In this case, they claim that the word for at least one sexual organ has the same root letters and, therefore, when *racham* is used to mean love, it means love in a sexual context. Further, so the argument goes, since God would never bring two people together in order to commit fornication, this relationship has to be a same-sex marriage. However, inasmuch as God's created order is marriage between a man and a woman, it makes no sense for God to actually take two men - one a teenaged Jew and one a Gentile - and put them into a same-sex marriage. But, looking at places where romantic love is described, such as Genesis 29:32 regarding Leah and Jacob, a different word is used. The word is *ahab* (aw-hab') or *raheb* {aw-habe'}; a primitive root; to have affection for (sexually or otherwise):—(be-)love(-d, -ly, -r), like, friend (unlike with David and Jonathan, the context involving Leah and Jacob is definitely the romantic love such as occurs between a man and his wife).

A HOMOSEXUAL ANTICHRIST? - One of the dangers of interpreting single verses of scripture as the National Gay Pentecostal Alliance does to make the relationship between Daniel and Ashphenaz one of same-sex marriage, is that you risk engaging in what amounts to pure speculation. An example of this is found in a book that I once read, titled The Homosexual Delusion by an evangelist in the United Pentecostal Church (a denomination that does not handle this issue well). In that book, the author suggests that the coming Antichrist might be a homosexual. He bases his theory on Daniel 11:37

where this coming world ruler does not regard "the desire of women." But if you look at this in connection with Daniel 11:36, it is clear not that the Antichrist will be a homosexual but, rather, that he will simply have no regard for anyone or anything because he will magnify himself above all.

JESUS AND JOHN - To suggest that our Lord Jesus had a homosexual relationship with the Apostle John is too controversial even for many gay theologians (though I had once been brazen enough to suggest it). Yet, the theory has been put forth and is based on the fact that John was "the disciple whom Jesus loved" (John 21:20) and that John rested on Jesus' chest during the last supper. The problem with making this into a homosexual relationship is that the word translated as loved in John 21:20 is not the Greek word for sexual love or even brotherly love but, rather, the godly kind of love that we're all to have for each other. The Greek word is *agapao*, meaning to love (in a social or moral sense). It is with this kind of love that Jesus asked Brother Peter in John 21:15-16, "...lovest thou Me?" It is of this kind of love that Jesus spoke when He said in John 14:15, "If ye love Me, keep My commandments." The suggestion that Jesus and John were homosexual lovers is a prime example of how a lot of people read into things - read between the lines - and select their own meanings rather than simply read things and try to discern the author's meaning.

ROMANS 1:26-27 - Please refer back to the section in Chapter 2 titled The Idolatry Factor. Rather than being a proof text against homosexual behavior, I believe this is part of a larger section (Romans 1:18-32) that shows the consequences of humanity's initial walking away from God to serve idols and that it likely shows how same-sex attraction came to exist.

1 CORINTHIANS 6:9-10 AND 1 TIMOTHY 1:9-10 - The controversy around these two passages involves the translation of two Greek words in 1 Corinthians 6:9-10, one of which is also used in 1 Timothy 1:9-10. Those two words are *malakos* and *arsenokoites*. Pro-gay theology insists that these two words are mistranslated and, therefore, do not refer to either homosexual behavior or homosexual orientation. The King James translates *malakos* as "effeminate" and *arsenokoites* as "abusers of themselves with mankind" in 1 Corinthians 6:9 and as "them that defile themselves with mankind" in 1 Timothy 1:10. The NASB translates the two words as effeminate and homosexuals, respectively. Darby translates *malakos* as "those who make women of themselves" and *arsenokoites* as those "who abuse themselves with men." Young's Literal Translation renders them as effeminate and sodomites, respectively.

So, what do the two words really mean? *Malakos* means soft, i.e. fine (clothing); figuratively, a catamite (a boy used in pederasty). If the word is being used in the figurative sense, the general concept is one of a male who adopts the passive sexual role normally reserved for females but, specifically, it would refer to the young pubescent boys who allowed older men to perform anal sex on them and/or otherwise performed sexual acts on older men. This practice was considered as normal in Greco-Roman culture as heterosexuality is in modern Euro-American culture, and is a major theme in Plato's book The Symposium. Otherwise, we don't really know what Brother Paul would have meant by a word that means soft or fine as in fine clothing. It could very well mean effeminate in the sense of a male who behaves in a feminine manner (as opposed to simply having a soft voice or soft mannerisms). It could also mean someone who lives an opulent, luxurious lifestyle, though no reputable English translation indicates anything but a sexual connotation or a male playing the role of a female. It could also mean the boy used in pederasty. *Arsenokoites* is the combining of the words for male (*arsen*) and couch (*koite*). Obviously, we wouldn't translate the word as male couch. However, *koite* means more than just couch: it has a sexual connotation. According to Strong's Exhaustive Concordance, it means a couch; by extension, cohabitation; by implication, the male sperm. If *koite* was being used with *arsen* specifically in a sexual context, then it very likely means men who sexually cohabit with men. Since *koite* implies the male sperm, this person would be the man who performs anal sex on another man or, otherwise, plays the dominant role. *Arsenokoites* could also mean a man who simply lives a sexually promiscuous lifestyle, though that is unlikely since Brother Paul mentions both fornicators and adulterers in the same verse (1 Corinthians 6:9). Additionally, it could be the older man in the pederastic relationship. Taken together, *malakos* and *arsenokoites* most likely refer to pederasty or to males engaging in the passive and dominant sexual roles - the "bottom" and "top" - respectively.

JUDE 7 - The controversy here is over the phrase used in the King James and NASB, "strange flesh." I mentioned this verse briefly in the section on the sin of Sodom as indicating either cannibalism or bestiality. The Greek words translated into this phrase are *heteros* and *sarx*. Young's Literal Translation is the only English-language translation I've seen that actually translates these two words correctly into the phrase "other flesh." *Heteros*, from which we get the English words heterosexual (ity) and heterogeneous (and its forms), simply means other or different. *Sarx*, on the other hand, is more complicated. Its primary meaning is flesh (as stripped of the skin), i.e. (strictly) the meat of an animal (as food). However, it has other meanings as well: by extension, the body (as opposed to the soul (or spirit), or as the symbol of what is external, or as the means of kindred), or (by implication) human nature (with its frailties [physically or morally] and passions), or (specially), a human being (as such). Again, I'm inclined to translate literally and, so, I think it is referring to meat. I think that since *sarx* can also mean human bodies, the phrase "other flesh" refers to cannibalism. A sexual connotation to *sarx* is less likely but, in such a case, I think "other flesh" would then be a reference to bestiality. The evidence is insufficient to support an interpretation that "other flesh" refers to homosexuality. *Sarx* is used in several passages in the New Testament in various contexts (Matthew 16:16; 19:5-6; 24:22; 26:41; Luke 24:39; John 1:13-14; 3:6; 6:52; 8:15, and 129 other times in addition to Jude 7).

Now that we've examined what the scriptures say about homosexuality, what do we do with this knowledge? It is clear that homosexual thoughts, behaviors and lifestyles are sinful but what about same-sex attraction? As discussed in a previous chapter, same-sex attraction is not sin - or even temptation - but neither is it something that is part of God's created order. In the next chapter, we'll examine God's created order as it relates to sexual expression.

CHAPTER 6 - GOD'S CREATED ORDER

Many gay rights activists are clamoring for the right to have same-sex marriages given legal sanction. Others reject the whole notion of marriage as being "a tool of the patriarchy" meant to keep women in submission to men. Marriage is not a new concept but, rather, one that's been around since God created the first female out of the first male's rib and that male acknowledged the female as being, "bone of my bones, and flesh of my flesh" (Genesis 2:23). Moses tells us that because of this acknowledgment, "Therefore shall a man leave his father and his mother, and shall cleave unto his wife: and they shall be one flesh" (Genesis 2:24). What, then, is God's created order? It is opposite-sex marriage between a man and a woman.

When God created a "helper suitable" (Genesis 2:20 - NASB) for the first man, He didn't create another male. Rather, He created a female. The second chapter of Genesis explains in detail what in general the first chapter states was accomplished: that "God created man in His own image, in the image of God created He him; male and female created He them" (Genesis 1:27). I disagree with the presbyter of the National Gay Pentecostal Alliance who said regarding the first female that, before the fall, she was not even physically female as we understand it but, rather, became what we know to be female as a result of the fall. He based his theory on his belief that the phrase translated in the King James as "help meet" is *ezer k'negdo* and is a masculine phrase. He claimed that the word *ezer* (meaning "helper") is the masculine form and that the feminine form would be *ezrah*. He said that Hebrew has no neuter gender: every word is either masculine or feminine: that most nouns referring to people have both a masculine form and a feminine form, like "actor" and "actress" in English. Because of this, he claimed that God didn't say He would make an *ezrah* but, rather, an *ezer*. He also said that the second half of this phrase, *k'negdo*, means "as opposite him," that is, as a mirror image - a clone. He claimed that the *ezer* didn't become an *ezrah* until after the fall and became so only as a consequence of the first sin. So, he was essentially saying that God created "Adam and Steve" and not "Adam and Eve," and that "Steve" had a sex change operation after the fall to accommodate the "curse" in Genesis 3:16. When I looked up the word "meet," as used in Genesis 2:18 and 2:20, in my Strong's Exhaustive Concordance, I didn't find *k'negdo* but, rather, I found *ezer* and it means aid. The same word is used for "help" in that verse and, so, I take the King James phrase "help meet" as being expressed in Hebrew as one word: *ezer*. Hebrew words have a masculine and feminine form but the scripture is clear that God made man male and female and that He made them so before the fall. (For the record, I disagreed with the presbyter on this even when I was still serving in ministry in that denomination).

GOD'S CREATED ORDER IS OPPOSITE-SEX MARRIAGE

God's created order is opposite-sex marriage - marriage between a man and a woman. Sex itself is the physical expression of what it means to be married: the two becoming one flesh. Any sexual activity outside of opposite-sex marriage is looked upon throughout scripture as sin. Jesus went even further and said that even to look at someone you're not married to and think about how you want to have sex with that person is sin (see Matthew 5:28). We get our first indication that opposite-sex marriage is what God intended when Moses wrote in Genesis 2:24, "Therefore shall a man leave his father and his mother, and shall cleave unto his wife: and they shall be one flesh." Jesus confirmed this in Matthew 19:4-6, "And he answered and said unto them, Have ye not read, that He which made them at the beginning made them male and female, And said, For this cause shall a man leave father and mother, and shall cleave to his wife: and they twain shall be one flesh? Wherefore they are no more twain, but one flesh. What therefore God hath joined together, let not man put asunder." (A clear indication that what Moses wrote was divinely inspired [God-breathed]). The author of Hebrews further confirmed this in Hebrews 13:4 where he said, "Marriage is honourable in all, and the bed undefiled: but whoremongers and adulterers God will judge." Does this mean, however, that everyone is required to marry?

NOT EVERYONE IS CALLED TO MARRIAGE

The first 12 verses of Matthew 19 contain Jesus' primary teaching on marriage and divorce - a teaching, I might add, that is essentially ignored in most churches today. In a nutshell, Jesus taught that marriage was between a man and a woman and that marriage was for life. There was no valid reason for divorce, "except it be for fornication" (Matthew 19:9). Under the Law of Moses, a man could divorce his wife for any reason; but Jesus made it clear as to why God allowed Moses to establish such a broad standard in Matthew 19:8, "He saith unto them, Moses because of the hardness of your hearts suffered you to put away your wives: but from the beginning it was not so." This was a difficult thing even for the disciples to hear as they protested in Matthew 19:10, after Jesus allowed divorce for the cause of fornication, "His disciples say unto him, If the case of the man be so with his wife, it is not good to marry." It's a high standard that our modern sensibilities find to be untenable. Oh, how often I have heard the objections when I preached Jesus' standard from the pulpit: "But what about spousal abuse? What if the husband is a drug addict? What if the wife molests the kids? What if we just don't get along?" Sorry, folks, Jesus didn't make any exceptions other than for fornication: if you're married, you're married for life. Jesus went even further and said that if you are divorced for any reason other than fornication and you remarry, or you marry someone who is divorced other than for fornication, you are committing adultery (Matthew 19:9). The sin, then, is not in the divorce itself but, rather, in the remarriage while your ex-spouse is still alive. Now, if you wish to object, "Brother, you struggle with same-sex attraction: what could you possibly know about marriage?" go right ahead and object. But you're objecting to what Jesus said and not to what I said. I was in an opposite-sex marriage for almost five years, partly because I erroneously believed that it would cure me of my same-sex attractions. I ended that marriage for reasons not having to do with my same-sex attractions and for reasons other than fornication. Matthew 19:9 specifically prohibits me from remarrying as long as my ex-wife is alive. Were I to do so, I would be committing adultery.

Not everyone is called to be married. Notice what Jesus said in response to the disciples' objection to the standard for divorce. In Matthew 19:11-12, He said, "All men cannot receive this saying, save they to whom it is given. For there are some eunuchs, which were so born from their mother's womb: and there are some eunuchs, which were made eunuchs of men: and there be eunuchs, which have made themselves eunuchs for the kingdom of heaven's sake. He that is able to receive it, let him receive it." Now, eunuchs were fairly common in ancient times but the context of what Jesus said suggests that He wasn't just talking about men who have been castrated and placed in charge of harems. Nor was He only talking about boys who were born with undescended testicles (something that may not have been medically correctable in those days) or who were otherwise impotent. I believe that Jesus was talking about three different groups of males: 1) those born with undescended testicles; 2) males who have been castrated and; 3) males who chose to remain unmarried and to live a life of celibacy. The Greek word translated here as eunuchs is *eunouchos*. It has a variety of meanings: a castrated person (such being employed in Oriental bed-chambers); by extension an impotent or unmarried man; by implication, a chamberlain (state-officer). When I was actively living a homosexual lifestyle, I took "eunuchs, which were so born from their mother's womb" to mean homosexuals - which I defined as people born without the capacity for sexual/emotional attraction toward the opposite sex. That may still be a valid interpretation but only in the sense that many Christian psychologists and pastors who minister to homosexuals in ex-gay ministries believe that there may be a genetic predisposition to same-sex attraction much the way that there is said to be a genetic predisposition to alcoholism. (I no longer believe that people are born homosexual or heterosexual, but there may be a genetic predisposition toward one orientation or the other). In any event, Jesus made it clear that there are those who are not called to be married. For the purpose of this book, I think we need to focus on the third category: unmarried males who choose a life of celibacy.

THOSE NOT CALLED TO MARRIAGE ARE CALLED TO CELIBACY

Brother Paul offered his own wisdom on the subject of marriage in 1 Corinthians 7. His views on the subject are rather controversial in some circles and may even be part of those portions of his epistles that Brother Peter said in 2 Peter 3:16 were, "things hard to be understood." It is also clear, however hard they are to understand, that Brother Paul's epistles had the authority of scripture according to Brother Peter. Let's take a look at 1 Corinthians 7.

"Now concerning the things whereof ye wrote unto me: It is good for a man not to touch a woman. Nevertheless, to avoid fornication, let every man have his own wife, and let every woman have her own husband. Let the husband render unto the wife due benevolence: and likewise also the wife unto the husband. The wife hath not power of her own body, but the husband: and likewise also the husband hath not power of his own body, but the wife. Defraud ye not one the other, except it be with consent for a time, that ye may give yourselves to fasting and prayer; and come together again, that Satan tempt you not for your incontinency. But I speak this by permission, and not of commandment. For I would that all men were even as I myself. But every man hath his proper gift of God, one after this manner, and another after that. I say therefore to the unmarried and widows, It is good for them if they abide even as I. But if they cannot contain, let them marry: for it is better to marry than to burn. And unto the married I command, yet not I, but the Lord, Let not the wife depart from her husband: But and if she depart, let her remain unmarried, or be reconciled to her husband: and let not the husband put away his wife. But to the rest speak I, not the Lord: If any brother hath a wife that believeth not, and she be pleased to dwell with him, let him not put her away. And the woman which hath an husband that believeth not, and if he be pleased to dwell with her, let her not leave him. For the unbelieving husband is sanctified by the wife, and the unbelieving wife is sanctified by the husband: else were your children unclean; but now are they holy. But if the unbelieving depart, let him depart. A brother or a sister is not under bondage in such cases: but God hath called us to peace. For what knowest thou, O wife, whether thou shalt save thy husband? or how knowest thou, O man, whether thou shalt save thy wife? But as God hath distributed to every man, as the Lord hath called every one, so let him walk. And so ordain I in all churches. Is any man called being circumcised? let him not become uncircumcised. Is any called in uncircumcision? let him not be circumcised. Circumcision is nothing, and uncircumcision is nothing, but the keeping of the commandments of God. Let every man abide in the same calling wherein he was called. Art thou called being a servant? care not for it: but if thou mayest be made free, use it rather. For he that is called in the Lord, being a servant, is the Lord's freeman: likewise also he that is called, being free, is Christ's servant. Ye are bought with a price; be not ye the servants of men. Brethren, let every man, wherein he is called, therein abide with God. Now concerning virgins I have no commandment of the Lord: yet I give my judgment, as one that hath obtained mercy of the Lord to be faithful. I suppose therefore that this is good for the present distress, I say, that it is good for a man so to be. Art thou bound unto a wife? seek not to be loosed. Art thou loosed from a wife? seek not a wife. But and if thou marry, thou hast not sinned; and if a virgin marry, she hath not sinned. Nevertheless such shall have trouble in the flesh: but I spare you. But this I say, brethren, the time is short: it remaineth, that both they that have wives be as though they had none; And they that weep, as though they wept not; and they that rejoice, as though they rejoiced not; and they that buy, as though they possessed not; And they that use this world, as not abusing it: for the fashion of this world passeth away. But I would have you without carefulness. He that is unmarried careth for the things that belong to the Lord, how he may please the Lord: But he that is married careth for the things that are of the world, how he may please his wife. There is difference also between a wife and a virgin. The unmarried woman careth for the things of the Lord, that she may be holy both in body and in spirit: but she that is married careth for the things of the world, how she may please her husband. And this I speak for your own profit; not that I may cast a snare upon you, but for that which is comely, and that ye may attend upon the Lord without distraction. But if any man think that he behaveth himself uncomely toward his virgin, if she pass the flower of her age, and need so require, let him do what he will, he sinneth not: let them marry. Nevertheless he that standeth stedfast in his heart, having no necessity, but hath power over his own will, and hath so decreed in his heart that he will keep his virgin, doeth well. So then he that giveth her in marriage doeth well; but he that giveth her not in marriage doeth better. The wife is bound by the law as long as her husband liveth; but if her husband be dead, she is at liberty to be married to whom she will; only in the Lord. But she is happier if she so abide, after my judgment: and I think also that I have the Spirit of God."

Brother Paul is addressing a number of issues here. Among them: marriage, being single, being a widow or widower, and divorce. Regarding divorce, Brother Paul adds one additional valid cause. He cites the following example: there's a couple that got married while they were both unsaved. If, during the course of the marriage, the man or woman later comes to receive salvation and the unbelieving spouse chooses to divorce, then he or she may divorce and the believing spouse is then free from the obligation of the marriage. If the believing spouse remarries, he or she has not sinned by doing so.

It's clear that Brother Paul did not consider marriage to be a sin. However, he would have preferred that everyone be celibate as he was. He confirms what Jesus said in Matthew 19:11-12 that not everyone was called to be married and then explains this in more detail. So, you married couples in the Church need to stop asking the single brethren when they're going to get married. Stop trying to play matchmaker. You single folks need to stop obsessing over the fact that you can't seem to find a suitable person to marry. To paraphrase Brother Paul, all of you - married and unmarried - need to just knock it off right now and focus on serving the Lord in whatever marital status you presently find yourselves!

It disturbs me greatly, in the light of 1 Corinthians 7, that most of the nationally- and internationally-known ex-gay ministries seem to focus so much on getting those of us who struggle with same-sex attraction into opposite-sex marriage. They often point to such marriages as proof that a person has changed and is no longer homosexual. Let me state this clearly: being in an opposite-sex marriage makes you no more heterosexual than going to church makes you a Christian or going to Burger King makes you a cheeseburger. Marriage is a very serious matter, as Brother Paul indicates, and is not to be entered into lightly. I believe that those who struggle with same-sex attraction should not be in a rush to get married and should not be pressured to do so. We should make sure that we are in a place where we are no longer struggling with such attraction before we even consider marriage. Not everyone is called to be married and a single person should not be looked upon as inferior to those who are married. Again, stop trying to play matchmaker!

I titled this book Pure As He Is Pure because I believe that I am called to celibacy. Not just because I am divorced and am not allowed to remarry as long as my ex-wife is still alive but, rather, because this is something that the Lord and I have discussed as we were discussing my embarking on this journey to overcome my same-sex attraction. I believe that the goal for me in this journey is to do what Brother John says in 1 John 3:2-3, "Beloved, now are we the sons of God, and it doth not yet appear what we shall be: but we know that, when He shall appear, we shall be like Him; for we shall see Him as He is. And every man that hath this hope in Him purifieth himself, even as He is pure." A lot of it has to do with my having been, until September 2001, in bondage since I was a teenager to what I call mental lechery. I was unable to even look at another man whom I found to be attractive without then taking a mental image of him and using that to play out scenarios in my mind of how I would have sex with him. As I played out the scenarios in my mind, I would proceed to masturbate. Some of the images stayed with me from when I was in elementary school and I sometimes even recalled those images as I engaged in my mental lechery. (I don't care what anyone says: even if it only took place in my brain, it was still fornication). I know that there are differing views in the Church on whether or not masturbation itself is a sin but, for me at least, it was sin because I was doing it while in the process of mentally fornicating with others (that these others were also male is really irrelevant in this particular context). I have often been accused of living life inside my head and, to a large extent, the accusation is valid; but it was also the primary means by which I was able to endure much of what I suffered as a child. My mind was a safe, comfortable refuge in an unsafe environment. Let's take a brief look at celibacy as we find it in God's word.

The scriptures are clear that, regardless of whether or not we are married, we are to be sexually pure. Brother John tells us that if we have the hope of seeing the Lord and becoming like Him, that we *will* purify ourselves to the same extent that the Lord is pure. Now, how pure is that? Hebrews 4:15, talking about Jesus as our High Priest, tells us plainly: "For we have not an high priest which cannot be touched with the feeling of our infirmities; but was in all points tempted like as we are, yet without sin." We are to be so sexually pure that we do not commit sin. Concerning marriage, you can argue all you want about what kinds of sexual activity are appropriate between a man and his wife; but I'll leave that issue for others to resolve. The question that concerns us here is how this applies to those of us who are not married.

CELIBACY IS ABSTINENCE FROM SEXUAL ACTIVITY AND THOUGHTS

What does it mean to be celibate? Does it only mean that we do not engage in sexual activity? Given that the scriptures clearly state that the sinful thought is equal to the sinful act (see Matthew 5:28, for example), I don't think that celibacy is limited to abstinence from sexual activity. We must also abstain from sexual thoughts. We must be sexually pure both in body and in mind. I was no less living a sexually promiscuous lifestyle when I was engaging in mental lechery while being physically celibate (physically, in the sense that I was not having sex with other people - though masturbation is also a form of sexual activity), than I was when I was playing the stereotypical drunken heterosexual sailor in the Navy, when I was going to gay bars and letting guys pick me up for one-night stands or when I was having short-term relationships with other guys. I praise Jesus that He was able to bring me to the place where I could finally be set free from my bondage to mental lechery. Brother Paul dealt extensively with the issue of celibacy in 1 Corinthians 7 and I urge you to study that passage carefully. Whether you are permanently called to celibacy or not, for as long as you remain unmarried the scriptures command you to be celibate. You are called to be pure, "even as He is pure" (1 John 3:3).

But, where do we go from the point of being free from mental lechery and masturbation? If we're going to remain free, we must learn how to be sexually pure, "even as He is pure" (1 John 3:3). In particular, all of us who struggle with same-sex attraction must learn how to be sexually pure because doing so is essential for the healing of that attraction and for getting the victory over homosexual thoughts and behaviors. We'll discuss how to get the victory over same-sex attraction in the next chapter.

CHAPTER 7 - GETTING THE VICTORY

Part of my struggle in dealing with my same-sex attraction came about as I was exploring the claims of ex-gay ministries. I was trying to get someone to explain to me what the end goal was - what they hoped to accomplish by pursuing this process - as well as how to get to that goal and by what standard to measure success. It frustrated me to no end that I couldn't get anyone to give me a straight (no pun intended) answer. Well, the Lord is a patient dad and He allowed me to go through this period of frustration for a time - but only for a time.

I posted this both in Yahoo's Ex-Gay Men's Ministry club and in my Pure As He Is Pure group on AOL, and I think it is appropriate here.

"Sometimes the Lord has to just smack me upside the head.

"I was spending some time in the word and in prayer earlier this evening, and the Lord and I were talking about what He is doing to help me overcome my same-sex attraction. As many of you know, I've been getting bent out of shape over needing to understand "the process" before I actually put myself through it. Looking at it as a map, I'm at point A (a guy with exclusively same-sex attraction) and am trying to get to point B. One of the problems was that I didn't know where point B was, much less how to get there. This is where the Lord decided to just smack me upside the head.

"You see, the Lord sent me to the church that I'm attending specifically to deal with my same-sex attraction and all of the different things that are related to it but not obviously so. The Lord has my pastor pushing me in specific directions to do specific things because the Lord is using those things to help me get to point B. What is my point B? If you were going to answer "opposite-sex attraction," that isn't it. My point B is to heal from all the things in my childhood that make me not able to relate properly either to other males or to females. The things in my childhood that even now cause me to push people away because I was so often rejected as a child for being "different" in the various ways that I was (or was perceived to be) different. My point B is to be brought to the place where I become a whole, unbroken man. The things that my pastor is pushing me into, things like participating in the men's breakfasts, getting to know people in the church, interacting with them, participating in the Bible study and other church activities besides just the worship service, are all the route highlighted on the Triptik (if you're not familiar with that, Triptik is the name of the maps that the American Automobile Association gives out that has mapped out the best route to your destination from whatever your point of origin).

"Using the analogy of a puzzle, I once described part of my struggle with being solitary (one of those things that are related to my same-sex attraction but not obviously so) and my particular objection to the first six words of Psalm 68:6 (in the King James) as questioning where I fit in like a piece of a puzzle - fitting into my place part of the whole picture but not standing out. Then the Lord smacked me upside the head again and explained to me that the whole picture is the body of Christ and I stand out not when I am in my place but, rather, when the piece that is me is not there, when the piece is absent, when the piece is missing."

What the Lord seemed to be telling me was that I needed to focus on being made whole. He was telling me that the way that I'm going to deal with my same-sex attraction is to deal with all those other things in my life that caused me to be a human male who is damaged. He revealed to me that I need to learn how to relate properly to other men and to women, and to discover my God-given role as an adult male. Some will criticize this and say that we are not to focus on the past. Such a statement would be true but we do have to learn from the past to see how we got to where we are and so that we are not doomed to repeat it. In this specific context, I need to identify how I came to have same-sex attraction and obtain healing for the factors that caused that attraction.

So, what is the goal in becoming "ex-gay"? Is it to go from having exclusively same-sex attraction to having exclusively opposite-sex attraction? Is it to achieve a level of sexual purity at which sexual/emotional attraction is essentially eliminated? Neither? Both? I think that maybe the answer is different for each of us within a limited range. This seems to be what the consensus was from my communication with other guys who are going through the process of becoming "ex-gay." In previous chapters, we discussed God's created order as being marriage between a man and a woman and discussed the origin of opposite-sex attraction as being a direct consequence of the first sin - as being the "desire" in Genesis 3:16. We also discussed the further corruption of that desire (as a consequence of idolatry) as being the possible origin of same-sex attraction, based on Romans 1:18-32. Because of the origins of sexual/emotional attraction, I don't think the proper goal is to simply change from one kind of attraction to another - one consequence of sin for another. That doesn't mean, however, that we have to settle for retaining our same-sex attraction. Same-sex attraction, in particular, has specific causes that we discussed in Chapter 2. Overcoming the effects that those causes had on our lives will help us overcome our same-sex attraction and make us whole. I've read testimonies of those who have at least begun to have some attraction for the opposite sex while also experiencing a reduced attraction for others of the same sex. In my own life, I can tell you that the Lord was merciful to me by reducing my attraction toward other guys from the moment I began examining the claims of ex-gay ministries for myself at the Lord's direction (though I don't have a corresponding attraction toward women). Since I didn't really do anything except to obey the Lord, I claim this as a miracle. However, I know of a number of brothers in Christ who have only experienced such a reduction after years of working at it while involved in an ex-gay ministry. I would like to perhaps suggest that the goal should be according to the title of this book - to be Pure As He Is Pure. As we read in 1 John 3:3, "And every man that hath this hope in Him purifieth himself, even as He is pure." Of course, the ultimate goal, the final destination, is to be conformed to the image of our Lord Jesus Christ.

Whatever the goal, it must conform in all respects to the word of God. In previous chapters we discussed opposite-sex marriage as God's created order and discussed sexual purity through celibacy outside of marriage. With permission, I can tell you that if we focus on these things, and on the principles to be discussed in the rest of this chapter, the same-sex attraction will mainly take care of itself. So, let's discuss some important principles (not that there are ever unimportant principles) that I believe will give us the victory over our homosexuality - both the behavior and the attraction. The ex-gay ministry in which I participate in my church focuses on the sanctification process in which all Christians are to be engaged. I believe this approach to be a correct one. You will find that if you also apply these principles to besetting sins - pornography, for example - you will gain the victory over those as well. You should consider these principles to be basic, foundational principles upon which to build others that more specifically address various aspects of homosexuality, such as those addressed in the video available from Exodus International, Understanding Homosexuality: Roots And Recovery by Sy Rogers.

GODLY SORROW THAT LEADS TO REPENTANCE

Brother Paul tells us in 2 Corinthians 7:10, "For godly sorrow worketh repentance to salvation not to be repented of: but the sorrow of the world worketh death." Sorrow over what? Sorrow over our sin. Not because we got caught or because we were declared to be guilty but because our sins have hurt God. He who created us in His image to have a relationship with Him is emotionally crushed by our sins. That's why He went out of His way to reconcile us to Himself by coming to Earth, living among us as a human, and sacrificing Himself on the cross to satisfy the demands of perfect justice while making it possible for us to be reconciled to Him. The most often-quoted passage of scripture is John 3:16, "For God so loved the world, that he gave his only begotten Son, that whosoever believeth in him should not perish, but have everlasting life." Our sins have separated us from God and, because of our sins, we deserve to burn for all of eternity in the lake of fire. Nothing that we could ever do on our own could ever reconcile us to God. As Brother Paul said in Ephesians 2:8-9, "For by grace are ye saved through faith; and that not of yourselves: it is the gift of God: Not of works, lest any man should boast." That salvation is even possible is entirely out of the undeserved kindness, the unmerited favor, of God - this is grace. All that He asks us to do is, as He said in Mark 1:15, "...repent ye, and believe the gospel." Once we receive salvation, the Lord never repents of having giving us that salvation: the Lord never regrets having saved us.

Before we can even think about overcoming our same-sex attraction, we need to make sure that we are right with God. Sure, we can try to overcome the attraction through secular methodologies such as reparative therapy but we will only have limited success. We need to get right with God; and to do so, the first thing we need to do is recognize our need for Him. We need to recognize that we are separated from Him by our sins, such as the homosexual lifestyles we've been living. Once we recognize our sinful state, we need to be sorry for our sins and how they hurt God. If we don't have this godly sorrow, we need to ask God to cause us to have it. Why? Because it is this godly sorrow that, as Brother Paul tells us in 2 Corinthians 7:10, "worketh repentance to salvation." Having godly sorrow causes us to want to repent and, when we do repent, we receive salvation. This is true even for those of us who are Christians. After all, 2 Corinthians 7:10 was originally addressed to Christians.

I'm going to ask you to do something right at this very moment. Put your bookmark in this page, close the book, go off to some quiet corner alone, and get right with God. Do not delay another moment. Repent of your sins and plead for the forgiveness that He wants oh so much to give you. If you're not already a

Christian, receive salvation by doing what Brother Peter told the people in Jerusalem to do on that Pentecost morning just 50 days after Jesus died on the cross. In Acts 2:38 we read, "Repent, and be baptized every one of you in the name of Jesus Christ for the remission of sins, and ye shall receive the gift of the Holy Ghost." Be reconciled to Him. Truthfully tell Him that you will no longer engage in homosexual thoughts and behavior and will no longer live a homosexual lifestyle but, rather, that you want to live a life that is obedient to Him and that you want to have the victory over homosexual thoughts and behaviors. Surrender your same-sex attraction to Him and ask Him to heal you. When you have done that, return to this page and we'll continue.

RADICAL AMPUTATION

This is a concept that I learned from the Pure Freedom course that I took through an online ministry called Setting Captives Free (their website URL is http://www.setingcaptivesfree.com). While the course mainly dealt with pornography and masturbation, the principles taught in the course were equally valid in dealing with my bondage to mental lechery. This concept is based on something that Jesus said in Matthew 5:29-30, "And if thy right eye offend thee, pluck it out, and cast it from thee: for it is profitable for thee that one of thy members should perish, and not that thy whole body should be cast into hell. And if thy right hand offend thee, cut it off, and cast it from thee: for it is profitable for thee that one of thy members should perish, and not that thy whole body should be cast into hell."

Here's the principle: if it's a hindrance in your life, it's got to go. If you're wanting to get the victory over same-sex attraction, then you need to get rid of everything that is associated with the homosexual lifestyle that you were living. Cancel your subscriptions to [13]The Advocate and Out. Delete the links to the gay chat rooms and websites from your browser's favorite places. Cancel your memberships to gay organizations and get off of their mailing lists. Get rid of the books, the nude pictures, the gay-themed movies, the rainbow flags, the leather jock strap you wore in the last Gay Pride parade - and anything that symbolizes your association with the gay community and with being homosexual. You must radically amputate your connection to homosexual behavior and whatever gay lifestyle you've been living. Jesus said that if your eye offends - causes you to sin - pluck it out. If your hand causes you to sin, chop it clean off! He wasn't speaking literally of removing body parts but, rather, the body parts are representative of anything in our lives that hinders our walk with Him. My radical amputation also included surrendering my ministerial credentials and leaving the pro-homosexual Oneness Pentecostal denomination in which I served. We need to follow the example that we find in Acts 19:18-19, "And many that believed came, and confessed, and shewed their deeds. Many of them also which used curious arts brought their books together,

---

[13] Magazines that promote homosexual lifestyles.

and burned them before all men: and they counted the price of them, and found it fifty thousand pieces of silver."

HIDE HIS WORD IN YOUR HEART

If you ever doubt the value of scripture in your life, read Psalm 119 (yes, the longest chapter in the Bible). I'll go even further and suggest that you pray the entire Psalm. Read what King David said in Psalm 119:9-12, "Wherewith shall a young man cleanse his way? By taking heed thereto according to Thy word. With my whole heart have I sought Thee: O let me not wander from Thy commandments. Thy word have I hid in mine heart, that I might not sin against Thee. Blessed art Thou, O LORD: teach me Thy statutes." The first step after we've radically amputated all those things that connected us to homosexuality is to make God's word part of the very core of our being - make it as natural to us as breathing. Now, this isn't something that we only do once and then forget it any more than breathing is. No. This is something we will need to do for the rest of our lives here on Earth. King David, the man after God's own heart, the man who lusted after another man's wife and then had the man killed so that he could have her for himself, had later learned this very important lesson. If David had been paying attention to God's word, he would never have done what he did. Do you want to be pure as Jesus is pure? David says the way to do that is "by taking heed thereto according to [His] word" (Psalm 119:9). That phrase, taking heed, is the Hebrew word *shamar*. It is a primitive root; properly, to hedge about (as with thorns), i.e. guard; generally, to protect, attend to, etc. David is saying that we can cleanse our way by hedging that way about, guarding it, protecting it, according to God's word. In other words, we've got to have a mindset that is continually focused on the word of God and on being obedient to that word. When Jesus fasted for 40 days and nights in the wilderness, Satan came along and tempted him with food before anything else. Satan just loves to kick a man when he's down - to attack when a man's at his weakest! But how did Jesus respond? Jesus responded by quoting the scriptures. It is no accident that the only offensive weapon in our spiritual arsenal is "the sword of the Spirit, which is the word of God" (Ephesians 6:17). Jesus used it, Brother Paul told us to use it, and King David told us that obedience to it keeps our way clean. Jesus said in John 15:3, "Now ye are clean through the word which I have spoken unto you." Here's what Bible commentator Matthew Henry had to say about Psalm 119:9.

"Here is, 1. A weighty question asked. By what means may the next generation be made better than this? Wherewithal shall a young man cleanse his way? Cleansing implies that it is polluted. Besides the original corruption we all brought into the world with us (from which we are not cleansed unto this day), there are many particular sins which young people are subject to, by which they defile their way, youthful lusts (2 Timothy 2:22); these render their way offensive to God and disgraceful to themselves. Young men are concerned to cleanse their way - to get their hearts renewed and their lives reformed, to make clean, and keep clean, from the corruption that is in the world through lust, that they may have both a good conscience and a good name. Few young people do themselves enquire by what means they may recover and preserve their purity; and therefore David asks the question for them. 2. A satisfactory answer given to this question. Young men may effectually cleanse their way by taking heed thereto according to the word of God; and it is the honour of the word of God that it has such power and is of such use both to particular persons and to communities, whose happiness lies much in the virtue of their youth. (1.) Young men must make the word of God their rule, must acquaint themselves with it and resolve to conform themselves to it; that will do more towards the cleansing of young men that the laws of princes or the morals of philosophers. (2.) They must carefully apply that rule and make use of it; they must take heed to their way, must examine it by the word of God, as a touchstone and standard, must rectify what is amiss in it by that regulator and steer by that chart and compass. God's word will not do without our watchfulness, and a constant regard both to it and to our way, that we may compare them together. The ruin of young men is either living at large (or by no rule at all) or choosing to themselves false rules: let them ponder the path of their feet, and walk by scripture-rules; so their way shall be clean, and they shall have the comfort and credit of it here and for ever."

So, how do we do this? How do we take heed according to His word? How do we hide His word in our hearts that we might not sin against Him? We must have a regular diet of God's word. Just as we need the right foods in the right quantities, along with sufficient exercise, to keep us physically healthy, so also we need to read, hear, meditate upon, study, memorize, and obey God's word in order to be spiritually healthy. This is the only way. Remember the Hebrew word translated in Psalm 119:9 as "taking heed"? What does that word mean? It means to hedge about (as with thorns), i.e. guard; generally, to protect, attend to, etc. If you haven't started to do so, get into the daily discipline of reading, meditating upon, and studying the Bible, as well as the habit of memorizing scripture. When you do, ask the Lord to teach you (Psalm 119:12). Start attending a Bible-believing church where you can receive solid, Biblically correct teaching: preferably a church that has an ex-gay ministry (so that you can get more focused assistance in dealing with your same-sex attractions and so that you can meet others who have been where you are). The Exodus website listed in the resources section of this book can refer you to a church that has such a ministry.

TAKE EVERY THOUGHT CAPTIVE

In 2 Corinthians 10:5, Brother Paul tells us, "Casting down imaginations, and every high thing that exalteth itself against the knowledge of God, and bringing into captivity every thought to the obedience of Christ." I want to focus on the last 10 words of that passage, "bringing into captivity every thought to the obedience of Christ." This passage is part of a section in which Brother Paul is teaching about spiritual warfare (see 2 Corinthians 10:3-6). There's a battle going on for the control of our minds. Satan wants nothing more than to have absolute control over us. If he can control our minds, he can control our bodies. This doesn't mean, however, that if Satan has control we can use the timeworn excuse, "The devil made me do it." God didn't buy that excuse from Eve and He sure isn't going to buy it from us! The Bible is very clear that if Satan has control over us, it's because we gave him that control. The responsibility is still ours.

Jesus made it clear that a sinful thought is the same as the corresponding sinful act - that to think it is the same as doing it. Remember Matthew 5:28? There Jesus said, "But I say unto you, That whosoever looketh on a woman to lust after her hath committed adultery with her already in his heart." The heart, as used here, doesn't mean the organ in our chests that pumps blood and oxygen throughout our bodies. Rather, it is the center of our being. There are tribes in the South Pacific that use the throat to represent that center of our being (instead of accepting Jesus into their hearts, they accept Him into their throats). Either way, what we're talking about here is that which controls us. We know from a medical standpoint that it is the brain that directs all bodily and emotional function. Thus, Jesus is saying that if we look for the purpose of lusting (imagining the ways we want to possess the other person sexually), we're committing adultery with that person in our thoughts. As one who has tended to live life in his head, I have a great deal of personal experience with this as I was in bondage from my teen years to mental lechery.

So, what does Brother Paul mean when he tells me that I need to be, "bringing into captivity every thought to the obedience of Christ"? Very simply, he means that I am to wrest control of my mind from Satan and bring it to the place where it is 100 percent obedient to Jesus. How do I do this? By doing what King David said, "by taking heed thereto according to [God's] word" - by causing it to conform to the word of God. As Brother Paul wrote in Romans 12:2, "And be not conformed to this world: but be ye transformed by the renewing of your mind, that ye may prove what is that good, and acceptable, and perfect, will of God." We do this by reading, hearing, meditating upon, studying, and memorizing God's word every day.

KILL IT

Brother Paul tells us in Colossians 3:5-7, "Mortify therefore your members which are upon the earth; fornication, uncleanness, inordinate affection, evil concupiscence, and covetousness, which is idolatry: For which things' sake the wrath of God cometh on the children of disobedience: In the which ye also walked some time, when ye lived in them." To mortify means to kill, to cause to become extinct. Notice the list of things Brother Paul says we're to kill: "fornication, uncleanness, inordinate affection, evil concupiscence, and covetousness, which is idolatry." Fornication is the Greek word *porneia*. It means harlotry (including adultery and incest); figuratively, idolatry, and is any sexual thought or activity that is outside of God's created order of opposite-sex marriage. Uncleanness is the Greek word *akatharsia*. It means impurity (the quality), physically or morally. Inordinate affection is the Greek word *pathos* and means properly, suffering ("pathos"), i.e. (subjectively) a passion (especially concupiscence). Concupiscence is the Greek word *epithumia* and means a longing (especially for what is forbidden). Our same-sex attraction falls into this category since the Hebrew word for desire in Genesis 3:16 defines that desire as a longing. Covetousness is the Greek word *pleonexia* and means avarice, i.e. (by implication) fraudulency, extortion. Covetousness is specifically referred to here as being a form of idolatry, of making something your god other than God Himself. Let's look at this list in Colossians 3:5 as rendered in Young's Literal Translation: "Put to death, then, your members that are upon the earth - whoredom, uncleanness, passion, evil desire, and the covetousness, which is idolatry. The American Standard Version (which is not the NASB) renders it this way: "Put to death therefore your members which are upon the earth: fornication, uncleanness, passion, evil desire, and covetousness, which is idolatry."

The majority of the items on this list have to do with sexual desires, thoughts and behaviors. Throughout the New Testament we see the extreme importance placed on taking control of our sexuality and bringing it into conformity with the word of God and with God's created order for sexual expression. What Brother Paul is telling us here is that if it isn't in conformity with God's design then not only must it die, we must kill it. He says that the things on the list in Colossians 3:5 are not part of God's design and, so, we must kill them. This act of assassination is an essential part of our getting the victory over our homosexuality.

By killing the things on the list in Colossians 3:5, we are no longer doing them. Notice what Brother Paul says in Colossians 3:6-7, "For which things' sake the wrath of God cometh on the children of disobedience: In the which ye also walked some time, when ye lived in them." It is because of the things on the list in Colossians 3:5 that God's wrath comes upon those who are "children of disobedience," meaning those who identify with disobedience or rebellion the way a son identifies with his father. But notice what Brother Paul tells the Colossian saints in verse seven: "In the which ye also walked sometime, when ye lived in them." Brother Paul is saying here, "Yes, God's wrath comes upon the children of disobedience because of these things that you yourselves used to be involved in when you were in that sinful lifestyle." In specific regard to our homosexuality, when we surrender all of who we are to the Lord Jesus and we kill all those sinful things in our lives, as well as the desires, the attractions, that lead us to sin, then it can be said of us that we walked in those things, we lived that homosexual lifestyle, but we don't anymore. So, as I mentioned in Chapter 1, when a lot of the folks in the ex-gay ministries say they are no longer homosexuals, they're saying that they don't walk in it anymore, they don't live there anymore. Satan will certainly try to bring them into captivity again by tempting them with sexually impure thoughts about others of their own gender; but because they have killed those things in their lives, they can victoriously overcome the temptations the way Jesus overcame His temptations: with the word of God. They confess what Brother Paul said about the Corinthians in 1 Corinthians 6:11, "And such were some of you: but ye are washed, but ye are sanctified, but ye are justified in the name of the Lord Jesus, and by the Spirit of our God." But, before they could do that, they had to do what Brother Paul tells us to do: they had to kill all those things in their lives having to do with their homosexuality.

THINK ON THESE THINGS

It is a Biblical truth that whenever God tells us not to do something, He gives us something to do in its place. In Philippians 4:8, Brother Paul wrote to the saints in Philippi, "Finally, brethren, whatsoever things are true, whatsoever things are honest, whatsoever things are just, whatsoever things are pure, whatsoever things are of good report; if there be any virtue, and if there be any praise, think on these things." As we get the victory over homosexuality, it isn't enough that we stop thinking gay-themed thoughts: we have to learn to think godly thoughts. We need to think thoughts that are true, honest, just, pure, of good report; things that are virtuous and praiseworthy. The Lord doesn't just tell us what not to do, He gives us something to do in its place.

Of all people, we Americans particularly detest being told what to think and told we have to surrender to authority. The right to our opinions, and to openly express those opinions, as well as the right to our individual liberty, is sacred in American culture - or so we like to believe. In reality, American society in the form of popular culture is constantly telling us what to think and what to believe. Even in this modern era of political correctness, we talk about celebrating diversity and differentness but draw the line when it comes to Bible-believing Christians or those who oppose diversity and differentness. It's as if American society is saying, "We will celebrate your diversity and differentness as long as you agree with us." It is one of the great contradictions of American culture: we celebrate individuality and independence but insist on conformity to cultural norms and values. But enough of the sociology lesson: what does this have to do with Philippians 4:8 and our getting the victory over homosexuality?

Brother Paul was writing some final thoughts as he concluded his letter to the church at Philippi. In one sentence - one that grammarians might consider a run-on sentence - Brother Paul tells us how to think: not merely the content but the character as well. He gives us a list of things that should characterize our thought life. Let's take a look at each item on the list individually.

1. **Whatsoever things are true** - Brother Paul tells us that our thoughts need to be accurate and that the things we think about are accurate. There are many folks out there, some of them calling themselves Christians, who think that humans evolved either from apes or from lower forms of life. We know from God's word that such a thought is not accurate. We were created, not evolved; we were made in the image and likeness of God, not the product of billions of years of random mutations affected by the environment. So, the first characteristic of our thought life is that the thoughts must be true. Thinking that we were born homosexual and can't do anything about it, thinking that we must embrace our homosexuality in order to be true to ourselves: these are things that are not true. We were not born with same-sex attraction: we may have been born with a predisposition toward such attraction much like some folks are born with a predisposition toward alcoholism but we weren't born with our same-sex attraction. Additionally, the detestable practice of homosexual men referring to each other in the feminine is utterly contradictory to thinking thoughts that are true. Excuse me, but I am not your girlfriend and I am not Nancy or Mary. I am male, I have always been male, and I have always been quite content being male, thank you very

much. The only way any of us can be true to ourselves and think true thoughts is when we surrender every part of ourselves to the Lord Jesus Christ and allow Him conform us to His image (see Romans 8:29).

2. **Whatsoever things are honest** - The Greek word possibly mistranslated here as honest is *semnos* and means venerable. It is rendered in the King James as grave (of serious demeanor) and honest. We are to think about things that are worthy of veneration, that are honorable. I don't know why the King James translators insisted on using words such as honest and honesty or grave and gravity where venerable or venerableness should be used, but if we're going to be able to think on those things that are true and venerable about the word of God, we need to translate the scriptures accurately. Though, perhaps this is yet another example of an English word (honest) that has a different meaning today than it had when it was used in translating the King James. But, that's getting off the topic. Thinking about things that are venerable or honorable (the words are nearly synonymous) means that we think about things that are worthy of reverence or respect. So, the second characteristic of our thought life is that the thoughts must be venerable. Thinking about sexual activity that does not conform to God's created design, thinking about the gay political agenda that seeks to redefine marriage and the family, thinking about the right to

"sexual freedom" is not thinking about things that are honorable.

3. **Whatsoever things are just** - The black community (sorry, I don't believe in hyphenated Americans: if we're citizens of the United States of America, we're all just plain old Americans) in Los Angeles during the trial of those police officers charged with beating Rodney King chanted the mantra, "No justice: no peace." They insisted that if they were not going to receive what they believed to be justice, that there would be no peace between the black community and the city of Los Angeles as a whole. It was, in effect, a threatened declaration of war. And, sure enough, when the verdict came acquitting the officers, many in the black community rioted. I was living in the El Cajon valley east of San Diego at the time and the rioting spread as far south as Highway 15 in the northern part of San Diego County. But what does it mean to think about things that are just? It means that we think about situations such as the one I mentioned here and develop a just (the Lord's standard of just) view of them. So, the third characteristic of our thought life is that it is to be just.

4. **Whatsoever things are pure** - There is some contention among homosexuals who call themselves Christian about sexual purity. Many of them seem to think that, because they are homosexual, the scriptural admonitions to be

sexually pure don't apply to them. The passage that says, "Whosoever looketh on a woman to lust after her hath committed adultery with her already in his heart" (Matthew 5:28) doesn't apply to them but, rather, only applies to married heterosexual men. While they will deny it, their actions and beliefs confirm exactly what anti-homosexual groups say about them: that their lives revolve around sex. I have visited so-called "gay Christian" chat rooms and I could not tell a difference between those rooms and non-Christian rooms. It horrified me when a former member of the Metropolitan Community Church (the largest homosexual denomination) told me how host churches were expected to fix guest ministers up with sexual partners during their visits. The presbyter of my former pro-homosexual Oneness Pentecostal denomination once told me that it's okay to think sexual thoughts as a tool for masturbation because what we're thinking about is only a fantasy and not the same as actually looking at a real person; and that masturbation was a proper means of sexual release. Yet, the scriptures tell us to be pure. Now, purity doesn't apply only to sexuality but that is the general context in which the term is used. The Greek word used in Philippians 4:8 for pure is *hagnos* and properly means clean. It is translated in the King James as chaste, clean and pure. It not only applies to behavior but, as we see in Philippians 4:8, to our thoughts as well. So, the fourth characteristic of our thought life is that it is to be pure.

5. **Whatsoever things are lovely** - Now this isn't exactly a word that "real men" in American society would use. It is, however, a commonly used word in Britain (we must remember that the King James was translated into English in Britain). Philippians 4:8 is the only place in the New Testament where the word is used. The Greek word that was translated as lovely is *prosphiles* and means to be friendly toward. It is a presumed compound of *pros* (toward) and *phileo* (the Greek word for brotherly love or love between friends). Thus, we're to think about things that are lovely - friendly - as opposed to thinking ugliness, bitterness, hatred, etc. So, the fifth characteristic of our thought life is that it is to be lovely. We are not, contrary to the pro-homosexual hymn sung in the Unitarian Universalist Church, "a gentle, angry people" and have no business trying to be. Rather, we are to be friendly people whose thought lives are characterized by lovely thoughts.

6. **Whatsoever things are of good report** - The Greek word translated into the phrase good report is *euphemos* and means something that is well spoken of. It is much like the English word reputable. We must think about things that are well spoken of, things that are of good reputation. Thus, gossip and thinking/saying bad things about people have no place in the life of a Christian. There is no place for the kind of queeny camp that so many homosexual men engage in. As Brother

Paul said in 1 Corinthians 13:5, love "thinketh no evil." So, the sixth characteristic of our thought life is that it is to be of good report.

7. **If there be any virtue, and if there be any praise** - When I think of virtue, I think of the woman in Proverbs 31. Here's a wonderful example of someone who has her act together and manages her affairs well. We would all do well, men and women, to follow her example. Other than in the gospels, the word virtue in the New Testament is a quality of character. I agree with Brother Albert Barnes who, in his Notes On The New Testament said, "Paul did not suppose that he had given a full catalogue of the virtues, which he would have cultivated. He therefore adds, that if there was anything else that had the nature of true virtue in it, they should be careful to cultivate that also. The Christian should be a pattern and example of every virtue…Anything worthy of praise, or that ought to be praised." So, the final characteristics of our thought life are to be anything that is virtuous and praiseworthy.

We cannot ignore the thought life. Jesus took the thought life so seriously that he said even the thought of having sex with someone to whom you were not married was the same as if you had actually had sex with that person (Matthew 5:28). Brother Paul tells us in 2 Corinthians 10:4-5 that, "the weapons of our warfare are not carnal, but mighty through God to the pulling down of strong holds; casting down imaginations, and every high thing that exalteth itself against the knowledge of God, and bringing into captivity every thought to the obedience of Christ." Every thought we think is to be in obedience to the Lord Jesus. We are to gain the mastery not only over our behavior and words (see James 3:2-18) but over our thought life as well. If there is any place where Satan can get the advantage over us if we're not careful, it is in our thoughts. This is where the temptation to sin takes place, not in our external body parts. This is where we will either escape the temptation (see 1 Corinthians 10:13) or be drawn away and enticed by our own desires (see James 1:14-15). There is a good reason for our thought lives to be characterized by the list in Philippians 4:8 - having such characteristics guard against temptation and, therefore, is a means of preventing sin. Controlling our thought life and bringing it into obedience to the word of God is a key element in getting the victory over our homosexuality and healing our same-sex attraction.

WALK IN THE SPIRIT

Brother Paul told the Galatian saints in Galatians 5:16-25, "This I say then, Walk in the Spirit, and ye shall not fulfil the lust of the flesh. For the flesh lusteth against the Spirit, and the Spirit against the flesh: and these are contrary the one to the other: so that ye cannot do the things that ye would. But if ye be led of the Spirit, ye are not under the law. Now the works of the flesh are manifest, which are these;

adultery, fornication, uncleanness, lasciviousness, idolatry, witchcraft, hatred, variance, emulations, wrath, strife, seditions, heresies, envyings, murders, drunkenness, revellings, and such like: of the which I tell you before, as I have also told you in time past, that they which do such things shall not inherit the kingdom of God. But the fruit of the Spirit is love, joy, peace, longsuffering, gentleness, goodness, faith, meekness, temperance: against such there is no law. And they that are Christ's have crucified the flesh with the affections and lusts. If we live in the Spirit, let us also walk in the Spirit."

Talk about stating the obvious! But sometimes we need to have things told to us with such brutal simplicity. How much clearer do we need it to be than, "This I say then, Walk in the Spirit, and ye shall not fulfil the lust of the flesh"? What is the flesh? The Greek word here is the same one that is used in Jude 7: *sarx*. The word means flesh (as stripped of the skin), i.e. (strictly) the meat of an animal (as food), or (by extension) the body (as opposed to the soul (or spirit), or as the symbol of what is external, or as the means of kindred), or (by implication) human nature (with its frailties (physically or morally) and passions), or (specially), a human being (as such). In the context of Galatians 5:16, it means the human nature that has this unnatural bent toward sin (there is nothing natural after the fall - everything is corrupted or tainted by the effects of sin). Brother Paul is telling us that if we walk, live our lives, in the ways of God, if we abide in Him and let Him abide in us, we won't bring about the longings of our sinful human nature, we won't engage in them, we won't live a sinful lifestyle. If you want to keep from doing what's wrong, Brother Paul is saying to do what's right. If you want to get the victory over homosexuality, stop living a homosexual lifestyle and stop giving in to homosexual desires. Instead, walk in the Spirit - walk in the ways of God.

Thankfully, Brother Paul didn't stop at stating the obvious. He went on to explain the battle that rages within the Christian between the Holy Ghost that dwells in us and our old unnatural bent toward sin. Look at Galatians 5:17-18, "For the flesh lusteth against the Spirit, and the Spirit against the flesh: and these are contrary the one to the other: so that ye cannot do the things that ye would. But if ye be led of the Spirit, ye are not under the law." The Greek word translated here as lusteth means to set the heart upon. So, when he says the flesh lusteth against the Spirit, Brother Paul means that our unnatural bent toward sin sets its heart against God's nature that dwells in us as the Holy Ghost. Notice, "and these are contrary the one to the other: so that ye cannot do the things that ye would." Our old unnatural bent toward sin wants to sin. The Holy Ghost dwelling within us gives us the desire to do the things that are pleasing to God. These two desires compete against each other for control. But then Brother Paul says something that is perhaps difficult to understand. Look at verse 18, "But if ye be led of the Spirit, ye are not under the law." What does he mean? The Law of Moses was not for the righteous but, rather, for sinners. Brother Paul explains in Galatians 3:24, "Wherefore the law was our schoolmaster to bring us unto Christ, that we might be justified by faith." If we are being led by God's Spirit we no longer need the schoolmaster because we have Jesus Himself now as our teacher: the Holy Ghost leading us into all truth (see John 16:13). We are declared righteous not by obeying the Law of Moses but, rather, by faith. As we read in Galatians 3:6, "Even as Abraham believed God, and it was accounted to him for righteousness." Brother Paul made an almost identical statement in Romans 4:3, "For what saith the scripture? Abraham believed God, and it was counted unto him for righteousness."

After he explains the battle that rages within us and tells us that it's the Spirit that needs to win out, Brother Paul gives us a list of things by which we can know we are walking in the flesh instead of the Spirit. What's that old expression by Miguel de Cervantes that I could never understand? "The proof of the pudding is in the eating." The list is in Galatians 5:19-21, "Now the works of the flesh are manifest, which are these; adultery, fornication, uncleanness, lasciviousness, idolatry, witchcraft, hatred, variance, emulations, wrath, strife, seditions, heresies, envyings, murders, drunkenness, revellings, and such like: of the which I tell you before, as I have also told you in time past, that they which do such things shall not inherit the kingdom of God." Did you notice that the first four items on the list involve sexual thoughts and behavior? If you go back to Romans 1:18-32, you'll notice the prominent place that sexual thoughts and behavior have in humanity's walking away from God. You simply cannot walk in the Spirit if you are engaging in the things on this list. If you are living a homosexual lifestyle, you can't walk in the Spirit because homosexual behavior is contrary to God's created design for sex as the physical expression of what it means to be married: the two becoming one flesh. Even if you should happen to be celibate, if you are embracing your homosexuality and believing that there's nothing wrong with being homosexual then you are still engaging in works of the flesh because you are disagreeing with God about His design and purpose for your sexuality. No, we didn't choose to have same-sex attraction but we must choose to be healed of it if we are to walk in the Spirit.

Brother Paul contrasts the works of the flesh with the fruit of the Spirit in Galatians 5:22-23, "But the fruit of the Spirit is love, joy, peace, longsuffering, gentleness, goodness, faith, meekness, temperance: against such there is no law." Notice that Brother Paul said the **fruit** of the Spirit and not **fruits**. There is only one fruit here. We must have everything that is on this list: love, joy, peace, longsuffering (patience), gentleness, goodness, faith, meekness, and temperance. I get so tired of hearing people talk about having the fruits of the Spirit as if they get to pick and choose which items on the list they're going to have. "Well, brother, I guess I got me the joy and the peace and the faith but I just hate those homosexuals and I ain't never gonna have me no love for them. Gentleness and meekness are for women and sissies, not for good old boys like me. And temperance? Oh, no sir. Me and the boys, we like to set around an' have us a few cases of beer on Saturday while we're out huntin' or settin' around watching the NASCAR races on the

TEEvee." The fruit of the Spirit is the evidence that God's Spirit dwells in us and has control over our lives. The things listed in Galatians 5:22-23 **together** comprise that fruit, that evidence. If we're focused on walking in the Spirit, we're not going to act on our same-sex attraction. We're not going to sit around thinking that we'll never get the victory over our homosexuality.

Notice what Brother Paul says next: "And they that are Christ's have crucified the flesh with the affections and lusts" (Galatians 5:24). If we belong to Jesus, we will have brutally killed our unnatural bent toward sin with all of its passions and desires. Our unnatural bent toward sin is not only contrary to God's nature but also to the nature that humans had before the first sin. It is not natural for humans to sin. It horrendously and brutally violates our created nature the way the men of Gibeah horrendously and brutally violated the Levite's concubine in Judges 19. That's just how serious this matter of walking in the Spirit is for the Christian. As Brother Paul summarizes in Galatians 5:25, "If we live by the Spirit, let us walk also by the Spirit." If we give our lives to the Spirit's control then we need to behave accordingly. That means we're not going to even entertain, much less do, the works of the flesh. Homosexuality, even though we didn't choose to have same-sex attraction, is a work of the flesh. We can't get the victory over it if we still allow it to have a place in our lives. We must take it captive, radically amputate it, and mortify it by crucifixion.

These are the principles by which we will get the victory over our homosexuality. We can't, however, do it alone. We need our brothers and sisters in Christ within the local church to emulate proper relationships between men and women, between men, and between women. We need saints who will agree to hold us accountable for our progress on this journey. The ex-gay ministries call such people our accountability partners. If you're a man struggling with same-sex attraction, find a godly man in your local church who is mature in the faith and ask him to hold you accountable - to ask how you're doing with prayer, reading the word of God, with getting rid of sexual thoughts, lusts, masturbation, etc., and to chastise you when you are straying into dangerous territory. Ladies, you need to find a godly woman of mature faith who will likewise hold you accountable as you learn to be the women in Proverbs 31 and Titus 2. We have same-sex attraction because we have been damaged as children. We need to repair the damage. This is where being part of a local church and interacting with godly men and women becomes so important. If you've been isolating yourself, as I have tended to do, you need to form friendships with others of your own gender so that you can learn how to be a godly man or woman.

CHAPTER 8 - BUT WHAT IF I FALL?

I wish that I could say that you will never again be tempted to engage in homosexual behavior or in other sins. Unfortunately, we live under a different reality: one where the closer we get to the Lord the harder Satan tries to get us to fall. Remember that battle that rages between the flesh and the Spirit? Satan is the one who is lending support to our flesh much in the way the Taliban have been supporting the terrorism of Osama bin Laden and his organization Al Qaida. Satan does not accept defeat easily. That's why we must learn from Jesus the way to defeat our enemies (the world, the flesh and Satan) as He did. As we're reminded in Hebrews 4:15, "For we have not an high priest which cannot be touched with the feeling of our infirmities; but was in all points tempted like as we are, yet without sin." But, let's say that you find yourself giving in to temptation. What do you do?

We have all the help we need to overcome temptation. 1 Corinthians 10:13 says, "There hath no temptation taken you but such as is common to man: but God is faithful, who will not suffer you to be tempted above that ye are able; but will with the temptation also make a way to escape, that ye may be able to bear it." We don't have to sin but we all-too-often find ourselves doing exactly that. Even Brother Paul struggled with temptation. He wrote about this struggle in Romans 7.

"Know ye not, brethren, (for I speak to them that know the law,) how that the law hath dominion over a man as long as he liveth? For the woman which hath an husband is bound by the law to her husband so long as he liveth; but if the husband be dead, she is loosed from the law of her husband. So then if, while her husband liveth, she be married to another man, she shall be called an adulteress: but if her husband be dead, she is free from that law; so that she is no adulteress, though she be married to another man. Wherefore, my brethren, ye also are become dead to the law by the body of Christ; that ye should be married to another, even to him who is raised from the dead, that we should bring forth fruit unto God. For when we were in the flesh, the motions of sins, which were by the law, did work in our members to bring forth fruit unto death. But now we are delivered from the law, that being dead wherein we were held; that we should serve in newness of spirit, and not in the oldness of the letter. What shall we say then? Is the law sin? God forbid. Nay, I had not known sin, but by the law: for I had not known lust, except the law had said, Thou shalt not covet. But sin, taking occasion by the commandment, wrought in me all manner of concupiscence. For without the law sin was dead. For I was alive without the law once: but when the commandment came, sin revived, and I died. And the commandment, which was ordained to life, I found to be unto death.   For sin, taking occasion by the commandment, deceived me, and by it slew me. Wherefore the law is holy, and the commandment holy, and just, and good. Was then that which is good made death unto me? God forbid. But sin, that it might appear sin, working death in me by that which is good; that sin by the commandment might become exceeding sinful. For we know that the law is spiritual: but I am carnal, sold under sin. For that which I do I allow not: for what I would, that do I not; but what I hate, that do I. If then I do that which I would not, I consent unto the law that it is good. Now then it is no more I that do it, but sin that dwelleth in me. For I know that in me (that is, in my flesh,) dwelleth no good thing: for to will is present with me; but how to perform that which is good I find not. For the good that I would I do not: but the evil which I would not, that I do. Now if I do that I would not, it is no more I that do it, but sin that dwelleth in me. I find then a law, that, when I would do good, evil is present with me. For I delight in the law of God after the inward man: But I see another law in my members, warring against the law of my mind, and bringing me into captivity to the law of sin which is in my members. O wretched man that I am! who shall deliver me from the body of this death? I thank God through Jesus Christ our Lord. So then with the mind I myself serve the law of God; but with the flesh the law of sin."

If you're a Christian, you know that when we come to the Lord and receive salvation, the Spirit of God comes to dwell in us and gives us the desire to do what is pleasing to Him. Yet, our old unnatural bent toward sin, referred to in scripture as the flesh and as our sinful nature, still wants to sin. However, we are no longer slaves to sin. Because of God's own Spirit dwelling in us we now have the ability to obey Him and keep from sinning. Without His Spirit dwelling in us, we are incapable of obeying Him. As Brother Paul said in Romans 3:10-18, quoting from several Old Testament passages:

"As it is written, There is none righteous, no, not one: There is none that understandeth, there is none that seeketh after God. They are all gone out of the way, they are together become unprofitable; there is none that doeth good, no, not one. Their throat is an open sepulchre; with their tongues they have used deceit; the poison of asps is under their lips: Whose mouth is full of cursing and bitterness: Their feet are swift to shed blood: Destruction and misery are in their ways: And the way of peace have they not known: There is no fear of God before their eyes."

Our old nature wants nothing to do with God. Oh, we may pretend to seek Him by getting involved in different religions or some form of spirituality. We may even involve ourselves in a Christian church. In reality, though, we want to deal with God on our terms and not on His. Try as we might, we are incapable of being righteous. We are incapable of doing good by His standards. As Christians, however, we have a new nature within us - His nature - and it is only with that nature that we are able to obey Him. Even then, we still find ourselves sinning - missing the mark - not meeting His righteous standard. So, again, what do we do?

If a Christian falls, it doesn't mean that he or she is down for the count. Yes, it's your own fault for falling. Yes, you are guilty. However, King Solomon tells us in Proverbs 24:16, "For a just man falleth seven times, and riseth up again: but the wicked shall fall into mischief." Psalm 37:23-24 tells us, "The steps of a good man are ordered by the LORD: and he delighteth in his way. Though he fall, he shall not be utterly cast down: for the LORD upholdeth him with his hand." If we are walking in the Spirit, the Lord directs our steps. His promise is that if we should happen to fall (as we are likely to do when we are resisting His direction), He is there to pick us up again.

The principles discussed in the previous chapter will help you get the victory over homosexual sin and help to heal your same-sex attraction. But if you should fall, know that all does not have to be lost. Know also that you don't have to go all the way back to the beginning and start over. Get back up again, repent of your sin, and continue on the journey walking with Jesus. Even before you get to that point, however, you have a source of help when you are feeling overwhelmed by the enemy's attacks: you can cry out to Jesus. As Psalm 40:17 tells us: "But I am poor and needy; yet the Lord thinketh upon me: thou art my help and my deliverer; make no tarrying, O my God."

It's been a hard lesson for me to learn that I can't do everything myself - that sometimes I need help. I grew up in an environment where I've pretty much always had to fend for myself - physically, emotionally and spiritually. As I became an adult, it became a dysfunctional mindset where not only did I believe that I had to do things for myself but, when it was clear that I needed help, my mind would tell me that I had no business asking for help because if I can't do it myself then I'm trying hard enough. My mind would conspire against me and tell me how much of a lazy slug I am if I come across something with which I need help.

But, that's not what the Lord tells us. He knows that we can't do it on our own. He knows that we need help. So, He anxiously awaits our call. The old hymn tells us that, [14]"Central's never busy, always on the line, you may hear from heaven, almost any time" (the only time you won't hear from heaven is when, as the hymn says, "Satan's crossed your wire"). The Lord will receive our call 24 hours a day, seven days a week. Isaiah 55:6 says, "Seek ye the LORD while he may be found, call ye upon him while he is near." Brother Peter tells us in 1 Peter 5:6-7, "Humble yourselves therefore under the mighty hand of God,

---

[14] From the hymn The Royal Telephone by F. M. Lehman as found in the United Pentecostal Church hymnal Sing Unto The Lord © 1978, Word Aflame Press.

that He may exalt you in due time: Casting all your care upon Him; for He careth for you." If you fall, get back up again, dust yourself off, and continue on the way with Him. An excellent book to read on this subject is the old classic Pilgrim's Progress by John Bunyan. There are versions of this more than 200 year-old book in modern English but I recommend that you read it in the original to get a better sense of what the author is saying.

A TESTIMONY IN BRIEF

If I had to summarize my testimony of what the Lord has done into a few sentences, I would quote Psalm 68:6 in which King David professes, "God setteth the solitary in families: he bringeth out those which are bound with chains: but the rebellious dwell in a dry land." I was rebellious and my life was like the parchedness of a desert as I lived a homosexual lifestyle and occasionally viewed pornography. I was a slave to mental lechery and masturbation but the Lord brought me out of my captivity. But He didn't stop there. He didn't just set me free and leave me out there in that parched land. Rather, he set me into a family where I could be fed and nourished and cared for, and where I will be able to feed and nourish and care for others. Let Him do the same for you.

CHAPTER 9 - CONCLUSION

All that we've discussed in this book can be summarized by one passage of scripture. King Solomon said in Ecclesiastes 12:13, "Let us hear the conclusion of the whole matter: [15]Fear God, and keep his commandments: for this *is* the whole *duty* of man." We have but one thing to do in our lives on this earth: to fear (have the utmost respect and reverence for) God and keep His commandments. As we read in Deuteronomy 13:4, "Ye shall walk after the LORD your God, and fear him, and keep his commandments, and obey his voice, and ye shall serve him, and cleave unto him." And as Jesus said in John 14:15, "If ye love me, keep my commandments." If we do what He says to do, we won't have time to do what He says not to do.

Some who read this will perhaps question why I didn't go into more detail about pro-gay theology. Others may question why I didn't go into the political agenda of the gay rights activists. Still others might question why I didn't say anything about HIV/AIDS. Why didn't I? The reason I didn't get into these issues is because dealing with them at length doesn't help me in my struggle with homosexuality and it really won't help you either. Now that we've left the homosexual lifestyles that we were living, we need to go on to healing and victory. In that particular journey, it really

---

[15] Fear, as used here, means to have the utmost respect and reverence for God, not to be afraid or terrified of Him.

doesn't matter what the gay rights activists want. It doesn't matter all that much what pro-gay theology teaches. Finally, why do we insist on associating HIV/AIDS with homosexuality? HIV is a virus transmitted primarily through sexual activity and it doesn't affect only homosexuals (in many places around the world it is primarily being spread among heterosexuals). That virus causes AIDS; and while some of you may be living with HIV/AIDS or know someone who is, that has nothing to do with our journey. It is entirely separate from our journey even if you contracted the virus while living whatever homosexual lifestyle you were living. I am sympathetic to your plight but HIV/AIDS really is an entirely separate issue.

This book is not an in-depth analysis of homosexuality. It is not a psychology textbook. Particularly with regard to the causes of same-sex attraction, there are books and other resources available that go into greater detail. I encourage you to turn to those resources if you feel that you need more information. My intent here, besides sharing my own struggle, is to help you get started on the journey. Sometimes too much information at once weighs us down and causes us confusion: it will only hinder us.

So, what am I saying in writing this book? I'm saying that there were things that occurred in our lives during childhood that caused us to have a mental illness, a neurosis, called same-sex attraction. I'm saying that we chose to act on that attraction by engaging in homosexual thoughts and behaviors or, at the very least, by embracing that attraction as natural, normal, or God-given. I shared numerous examples from my own life in explaining both how same-sex attraction develops and how to get the healing and victory we need. I'm saying that healing and victory are not only possible, they are necessary. I saying that the ultimate goal, the destination in our journey is to be conformed to the image of our Lord Jesus Christ and to be pure, as 1 John 3:3 tells us, "even as He is pure." This process of conforming to His image is what scripture calls sanctification and is to be the goal of every Christian.

I encourage you to examine your own life carefully and see what things in your childhood caused your same-sex attraction. In fact, go to the Lord in prayer and ask Him to reveal these things to you. To be quite honest, I have yet to meet any man with same-sex attraction for whom at least some of the things discussed in this book were not factors. If you are not a Christian, I urge you to surrender your life to Jesus now. This book will not be of much help to you if you don't have a personal, growing relationship with the Savior. In fact, I believe you will only meet with limited success in your struggle to overcome your homosexuality without Him dwelling in you and being the absolute Lord of your life. That's the key to getting the victory over our homosexuality: our absolute and total surrender to Him and unwavering obedience to His commands. After all, He created us: He knows what's best and, unlike humans, He never fails or disappoints us. So, won't you surrender to Him? Won't you this day choose to "fear God and keep His commandments"? Won't you obey His voice and serve Him and cling to Him? Let Him love you, heal you and give you the victory.

RESOURCES

There are numerous resources available to help you in your struggle with homosexuality. The list below is of websites and other resources that you can go to for additional help. Some of them, such as the Exodus website, also have books available that deal with various aspects of the struggle as well as books that tell the stories of men and women who have come out of homosexuality.

EXODUS NORTH AMERICA - a clearinghouse for ex-gay ministries and other resources. Their website URL is http://www.exodusnorthamerica.org.

EAGLES' WINGS MINISTRY - this website has been a particular blessing to me as I was researching the claims of ex-gay ministries. It contains articles, testimonies and other resources. Their website URL is http://www.ewm.org.

NARTH - this is the website for the National Association for Research and Therapy of Homosexuality (NARTH). It focuses on the psychological causes of homosexuality and treatment through reparative therapy. Their website URL is http://www.NARTH.com.

GOD MADE THEM MALE AND FEMALE - another resource that was particularly helpful to me. This one focuses on celibacy. Their website URL is http://ourworld.compuserve.com/homepages/rossuk/AdamEve.htm

BUGGIN' OUT - this entertaining website contains testimonies and articles by men who are have come out of homosexuality and are on the journey toward healing. Their website URL is http://www.homestead.com/BugginOut/BugginOut.html.

WHO IS THIS GUY ANYWAY? - this is my personal website. It tells of my own struggle with and journey out of homosexuality. The website URL is http://hometown.aol.com/buddychan2/myhomepage/index.html.

PURE AS HE IS PURE - this is my AOL club for men who struggle with same-sex attraction. I started this group because I needed a place where I could go for encouragement and support and there was no such group in AOL (my Internet provider). The website URL is http://groups.aol.com/purelikejesus.

LAST DAYS MINISTRIES - this is the website for what used to be Brother Keith Green's ministry that is now headed by his widow, Melody Green. They have numerous free articles on a wide variety of topics, including homosexuality. Their website URL is http://www.lastdaysministries.org.

LIVING THE CRUCIFIED LIFE - This book, written by Ralph V. Reynolds, is an excellent book that will help the believer to live the kind of life reflected in Galatians 2:20, "I am crucified with Christ: nevertheless I live; yet not I, but Christ liveth in me: and the life which I now live in the flesh I live by faith in the Son of God, who loved me, and gave Himself for me." It is available from Alpha Bible Publications, P. O. Box 155, Hood River, OR, 97301.

UNDERSTANDING HOMOSEXUALITY: ROOTS AND RECOVERY - This video is one of the sessions of the 1995 Exodus Conference and is taught by Sy Rogers. It is available as part of Exodus International's Foundational Issues Series. You can purchase a copy through Exodus. In this teaching, Sy Rogers examines developmental factors, highlighting the interplay of biological, psychological and spiritual elements. He also addresses various aspects of recovery - what recovery is and isn't - and why it takes so long. This is must viewing for both the homosexual seeking to get the victory over homosexuality and those who minister to homosexuals.

SEXUAL HEALING - By David Kyle Foster. This reference tool is an excellent resource for those who want to help others trapped in sexual sin or brokenness, for those called to lay or professional ministry, and for those who struggle with sexual sin and brokenness. It offers a biblical approach from someone who has struggled and gained the victory. It is available through Mastering Life Ministries, P. O. Box 351149, Jacksonville, FL 32235-1149 or online at http://www.MasteringLife.org.

THE MEASURE OF A MAN - This classic work by Gene A. Getz is an excellent personal or group study on the attributes of a godly man. One of the issues with which most homosexual males struggle is masculine identity. While not written specifically for the homosexual, this book is an important tool that will help you develop a healthy, godly masculine identity. Most Christian bookstores carry this book or can order it for you. It is currently published by Regal Books.

These are by no means all-inclusive but from these you can find out about other resources that are available. If you're looking for an ex-gay ministry in your area, go to the Exodus website and click on the link for Find A Ministry.

ABOUT THE AUTHOR

Chancellor Carlyle Roberts, II was a welfare kid who ran the streets. He came to Christ when he was 13 but struggled in silence with same-sex attraction. After graduating from high school in 1981, he served in the U. S. Navy for 11 years during which time he walked away from the Lord. In 1993 while going through a divorce, he began living a promiscuous homosexual lifestyle and became an ardent gay activist. In 1995, he returned to faith in Christ through a pro-homosexual Pentecostal denomination, the National Gay Pentecostal Alliance. After completing that denomination's Bible school requirements, he served in pastoral, prophetic and teaching ministry. In August 2001, the Lord led him to explore the claims of ex-gay ministries and used that exploration to bring him out of homosexuality and put him on the journey toward healing and victory. He now participates in an ex-gay ministry in Buffalo, New York.

www.ingramcontent.com/pod-product-compliance
Lightning Source LLC
Chambersburg PA
CBHW022217050726
47590CB00002B/839